Organized Home:

Ideas and tips for decluttering your home, room by room, the better solution for organizing your house and life.

&

Home Cleaning Tips:

Tips and Techniques For Cleaning Your Home

© Copyright 2019 by Karla Moore - All rights reserved.

This content is provided with the sole purpose of providing relevant information on a specific topic for which every reasonable effort has been made to ensure that it is both accurate and reasonable. Nevertheless, by purchasing this content, you consent to the fact that the author, as well as the publisher, are in no way experts on the topics contained herein, regardless of any claims as such that may be made within. As such, any suggestions or recommendations that are made within are done so purely for entertainment value. It is recommended that you always consult a professional prior to undertaking any of the advice or techniques discussed within.

This is a legally binding declaration that is considered both valid and fair by both the Committee of Publishers Association and the American Bar Association and should be considered as legally binding within the United States.

The reproduction, transmission, and duplication of any of the content found herein, including any specific or extended information will be done as an illegal act regardless of the end form the information ultimately takes. This includes copied versions of the work both physical, digital and audio unless express consent of the Publisher is provided beforehand. Any additional rights reserved.

Furthermore, the information that can be found within the pages described forthwith shall be considered both accurate and truthful when it comes to the recounting of facts. As such, any use, correct or incorrect, of the provided information will render the Publisher free of responsibility as to the actions taken outside of their direct purview. Regardless, there are zero scenarios where the original author or the Publisher can be deemed liable in any fashion for any damages or hardships that may result from any of the information discussed herein.

Additionally, the information in the following pages is intended only for informational purposes and should thus be thought of as universal. As befitting its nature, it is presented without assurance regarding its prolonged validity or interim quality. Trademarks that are mentioned are done without written consent and can in no way be considered an endorsement from the trademark holder.

Table of Contents

Organized Home: 1

Introduction 2

Chapter 1: Is Your Messy Home Weighing You Down? 4

Chapter 2: A Happy Home Is a Tidy Home 13

Chapter 3: Toss What You Don't Need 23

Chapter 4: Your Organizational Rulebook 33

Chapter 5: Less Clutter & Greater Freedom 42

Conclusion 52

Description 53

Home Cleaning Tips: 55

Introduction 56

Chapter 1: Go with Natural Cleaning Products 57

Chapter 2: Cleaning Kitchen Spaces 81

Chapter 3: Make the Bathroom Sparkle 94

Chapter 4: General Living Spaces 104

Chapter 5: Dining Area 110

Chapter 6: Laundry Area 113

Chapter 7: The Children's Corner 116

Conclusion: A Final Word 121

Index 126

Description 132

Organized Home:

Introduction

Congratulations on downloading this book and thank you for doing so.

Here's a quick question to ask yourself: *Do you look forward to coming home every day?*

Or do you prefer to delay coming home as long as possible because you find yourself feeling stressed out by the one place that's supposed to be your go-to sanctuary after a long, hard day? If you do, then that's a clear sign that something needs to change. *Badly*.

Your home is your safe haven. The one place you can be yourself without any inhibition. The place where you're supposed to feel at your happiest because *this is what home feels like*. Every other environment may cause you to stress, but not your home. Your hope is your happy place. Unless of course, your home happens to be a chaotic mess that always looks like the aftermath of a disaster zone. That might explain why you'd rather be anywhere else but home, and no wonder since you probably feel stressed by your own mess.

Many people don't often associate stress with a messy home environment. It's just not something that we think about unless it's pointed out to us. Our brains are simply not wired to be happy in an environment that is disorganized. It simply isn't. Even if you think you've gotten so used to your mess that it doesn't bother you anymore, deep down it still does on a subconscious level. That's why you find it hard to relax at home when it's not as neat as it should be.

Your home should never be a place that contributes to your stress, and if it is, then perhaps it's time to get organized and start decluttering. You'd be surprised at how much those two words can inflict a profound difference in your life, once you start actively putting it into practice.

There are plenty of books on this subject on the market, thanks again for choosing this one! Every effort was made to ensure it is full of as much useful information as possible. Please enjoy!

Chapter 1:
Is Your Messy Home Weighing You Down?

Take a look around your home right now. What do you see? A comfortable, cozy space that fills you with warmth and happiness just by looking at it? Or do you see piles of clutter, junk, and mess collecting in various nooks and crannies around the house? Expired food in the fridge. Piles of letters, mail, and magazines in one corner. Closets were bursting full of clothes. Papers, documents, and stacks of books in another. The chances are that there is at least one area or more around your home that is just piled with far too much stuff and lacking any kind of organization.

Who would have thought that the amount of clutter that's sitting in your home right now could have such a deep emotional and psychological impact? After all, they're just piles of stuff, right? What could be so bad about having stuff? But the thing is, clutter has a way of affecting you mentally and physically without you even knowing it. Being surrounded by disorganization makes it hard for anyone to concentrate. When it becomes impossible to have clarity in your life, you begin to question and wonder what you're doing with your life.

Too much clutter can weigh you down. The home that's supposed to be the one place you can always come back to and unwind, the place where you should be free to be yourself, has now become a place of mental and emotional chaos. Clutter causes a lot of negative impacts that we're not giving a second thought to, and if you can relate to any of the side effects below, your messy home is weighing you down more than it should:

- **You Struggle to Get Anything Done** - Productivity can be low when you're distracted by all the mess that is surrounding you. Not just at home, but at work too. A messy cubicle and work desk can make it hard to get anything done, even more so if you spend far too much time looking for items because you can't find them among the mess.

- **You're Not Motivated Anymore** - At all. Just thinking about cleaning the mess in your home leaves you feeling so drained that you lose your motivation entirely. That lack of motivation will slowly start seeping into and affecting other areas of your life, and while you may still be able to get away with it at home, losing motivation at work is never a good thing. No company wants to see an employee who is losing momentum and productivity, that's never good for business.

- **You're Even More Susceptible to Procrastination** - Clutter encourages procrastination. Each time you put off organizing your home, you're procrastinating. Each time you procrastinate, it gets harder to start moving again. When you're constantly putting off clearing and cleaning up until "tomorrow," that kind of thinking is going to develop into an unhealthy behavior pattern which is going to extend into the other areas of your life, and procrastination is never a good habit to have.

- **You're Always Tired and You Don't Know Why -** Being stressed out all the time will do that to you. You may think you're not stressed or bothered too much by the piles of clutter you see around you, but subconsciously you are. Some people just look at clutter and automatically feel tired at the very thought of having to work through the mess and clear it up.

- **Your Mess Makes You Depressed -** When all you see is mess surrounding your life, you can't help but sometimes feel hopeless, wondering how it came to this. These feelings will be amplified over time if nothing is done about the clutter, and as the clutter grows, so too do your feelings of misery and despair.

Why Keep Your Home Clutter-Free: The Benefits of a Clutter-Free Home

Do you feel it's time for a big life change? We all reach a point sometimes where we're tired of the routine that we have now because it no longer brings us any joy or contentment. You might have reached that point the moment you realized your home is not how you want it to be. Sometimes, it just hits you like a bolt of lightning. When that realization hit is when you know that something needs to be done to make a change for the better.

Your home would look a lot different without all the unused items which are taking up space. Imagine living in an environment that is simple, clean, and with lots of free space and surfaces. Imagine opening your closet doors and being greeted with a view that is simple and stress-free, where clothes are not being cramped and squished together and piled haphazardly on shelves.

Do you know that feeling that comes after you've given your home a good and thorough spring cleaning session? That happy, satisfied feeling of a job well done as you look around your home and dust your palms together admiring how much better your home looks and how badly it needed to be cleaned out. It's safe to say that you can immediately see a few benefits of having a clutter-free home, such as a more organized household, less cleaning, less stress, and probably less money spent unnecessarily on items that you don't need or want.

It's not an exaggeration to say that decluttering and organizing your home can be a truly life-changing experience. There are some people out there who have completely transformed the way that they live and the environment *they choose* to live in by opting to live as a minimalist. As the name implies, these individuals have organized their homes by choosing to remove everything except what is necessary for their survival, and they claim their lives have never been better. Even if you choose not to toss out almost everything you own and keep only the bare essentials you need, rearranging your belongings in a more orderly and tidy fashion can be just as beneficial until you reach a point where you're comfortable enough to get rid of items that you no longer need in your home.

Besides the more obvious benefits of what removing the clutter and the junk from your home can do for you, here are some other surprising benefits you stand to gain that you might not have thought about:

- **You'll Have More Space in Your Home -** This one goes without saying. The less stuff you have, the more room you've got. This is going to be the benefit that you're going to be able to visually observe the most. The fact that your house suddenly seems a lot more spacious when it doesn't have unnecessary piles of stuff cluttering every available corner. You'll feel lighter, more relaxed, and even a sense of satisfaction and having freed up all this extra space around you.

- **You Make Room in Your Life for what's Important -** When you're no longer drowning in clutter, you're better able to focus on what brings true value and meaning in your life. When we start purging out all unnecessary things out of our lives, whether it's non-physical or physical, we create space, and we also create peace. Once you realize that it's not your material possessions bringing you happiness, you start to look for happiness within you, which is what you should have been doing all along. Material happiness will never last as long as your internal happiness.

- **Ability to Focus More-** We all has a passion for something. Some have already found it while others are still searching for it. But when you're always stressed out by your home environment, it makes it difficult to concentrate on anything, let alone your passion. Being distracted and unable to focus on anything else except your stress is how you slowly start to burn out and feel demotivated over time.

- **You Feel Relieved** - Clearing away the clutter in your life is going to feel like a big weight has been lifted off your shoulders. Suddenly, you have room to breathe again once more. We often don't realize just how much we are affected by the clutter and accumulation of possessions around us until we get rid of it and feel much better when we've tossed out a few items.

- **You Learn a Life Changing Lesson** - You're learning a valuable life lesson when you start realizing that material possessions are not responsible for bringing you happiness.

- **A Change in Your Priorities** - Another big shift in your life is going to be the difference you notice in your priorities. As you begin decluttering, removing all that is unnecessary and not actively contributing to your happiness, your priorities are going to change in a good way. The things that you once thought the matter would no longer seem so important.

- **You'll be a Lot Calmer** - When you take the stress out of the equation, it's easier to feel a lot happier and calmer when every little thing is not getting on your nerves or threatening to set you off. Another happy side effect of decluttering is that life will become a lot less stressful when you have nothing left to stress you out.

Even More, Reasons to Keep Your Home Free of Clutter

Did you know that your material possessions, everything that you own and have in your home right now, are taking up a lot more of your time than you realize? Think about how much time you spend looking for items that seem to be "lost" because you can never find it in the mess? Are you spending several hours of valuable time which could be allocated towards other tasks trying to get your home looking presentable but failing miserably because the mess is just too much to deal with? All the material possessions you own demand a lot more of your time to upkeep then you realize.

- **You *Despise* the Cleaning Process**. Some people love it; others detest it. If you're in the latter category, then that's all the reason that you need to keep your home free of clutter. There's a lot less stress involved when there's less to clean, not to mention cutting down the amount of time you spend on the cleaning process itself.

- **You're Tired of Being Stressed by Your Mess -** We don't realize just how much stress the things in our life can cause us until we look around and ask ourselves *how on earth did I collect so much stuff?* Your external physical environment can contribute to the way that you feel, and if you need more proof, just think about all those times when you had to come home to a messy home. When you come home after a long day at work only to find a mess waiting for you at home, you get stressed. When you reduce the amount of clutter in your life, the stress that you feel is going to be significantly reduced, which in turn will help you feel more relaxed.

- **You Want to Rekindle Your Relationships** - By reducing the amount of clutter, you've got going on in your life, and you're taking away those distractions. What you get in return is the ability to reconnect and focus once more on the people who matter in your life and what's important. The less time you spend on the materialistic aspects of your life, the more time you have to spend on the ones who truly enrich your life and give it meaning.

- **You Want Your Savings to Improve** - Who knew there would be financial benefits to be gained by getting rid of clutter? Buying less material possessions means more money for you to put aside into building your savings nest egg. Especially if you've gotten into the habit of making purchases with your credit card. By simply buying less, you're saving more.

- **You Want to Become More Efficient** - Suddenly, when you have a lot less stuff in your life, you find yourself becoming a lot more efficient than what you were before. You will find yourself managing your time more efficiently with fewer distractions, and you won't feel as pressured as you once did before as a result of this. You will be able to accomplish more, feel more productive, and you won't feel as pressed for time as you want did before because there is nothing that is distracting you from what you should be doing.

Key Takeaway Points

One of the first few things you need to do to start cultivating a more organized home environment is to make a personal commitment to achieving this goal. Your commitment should be that from this day forward, and that's what you're going to stick to. Yes, it's going to involve a lot of hard work, depending on the size of your home, but the key here is to start small. Commitment is all about being dedicated to doing something, to act in order to bring out the desired result. It is the dedication to take action. The benefits that you ultimately stand to gain by not having a messy home that weighs you down is well worth the effort that you're about to put in as you discover over the next few chapters what it takes to organize your home and your life.

Chapter 2:
A Happy Home Is a Tidy Home

We live in a world today where it has become impossible not to be stressed. The hectic, demanding lifestyles we lead which constantly pulls our attention in all different directions, rushing from one task to another and having schedules so packed that it sometimes seems you don't even have a moment to stop to relax for a minute. Stress has become almost unavoidable these days, and the one place you should be able to go for some much-needed downtime after a long day is a comfortable home which invokes a sense of calm and peace. That can only happen though if your home is not another source of stress.

The Problem with Clutter and Why We Hold Onto It

Here's an interesting point to think about. America is home to about 3% of the world's child population. Yet, America is the country that purchases about 40% of the world's toys. Is it any wonder then that we find ourselves in a home that is messier than we would like it to be?

The answer is right in front of us. We live in a society today that's far too materialistic, and with social media and the constant, non-stop advertising that gets thrown in front of us, it can be hard to resist the siren call of temptation to just give in and buy, buy, buy. Ads convince us that we need more stuff to make us healthier, that we need to make more purchases to be considered successful, that the more we buy, the happier we will be because who can resist the thrill of owning something new?

We have become so conditioned to a life of materialism that we genuinely believe the decisions about the purchases we make are based on careful thought and sound logic, but in all honesty, that's far from the truth. There's a classic sales quote which sums up this scenario perfectly: *"People don't buy products. What they're buying is better versions of themselves"*. The purchases that we make represent our hopes, what we believed to be true when we bought them, and what we hope it will help us achieve down the road. We make purchases in the hopes that we will finally become a happier version of ourselves, the way those ads promised.

Because we hold onto that hope, decluttering becomes a difficult process for many to accept. Having to get rid of all that stuff you bought is like admitting you failed on some level. That despite trying, you still find yourself unhappy, miserable, and unfulfilled. Then, of course, there's that feeling of guilt at having to admit you wasted your money making those purchases, so you try your best to hang onto them to justify buying them in the first place. A lot of people are especially afraid of feeling regret. What if they were to toss out something now that they end up regretting down the road? What if they need it next time? Shouldn't they hold onto the items then "just in case"? This "just in case" scenario is going to trap you in in a never-ending cycle of debt.

Less Clutter Means Less Stress

Have you ever envied those beautiful pictures you see on online of homes that look so neat and tidy? Practically empty except for a few pieces of essential furniture, yet despite its minimal setup, it's still preferable to the space that you find yourself surrounded in now.

It may sound strange, but it's true. Too much stuff is bad for you, although advertisers work hard to make you believe otherwise. If you're not one of those people that find cleaning a relaxing affair, the seemingly never-ending clean-up process around the home is going to take its toll on your mentally and physically. But if having a lot of unnecessary stuff is bad for us, why do we feel the constant urge to keep buying more? There always seems to be a new want, a new need, or a new desire that needs to be fulfilled, tempting us to spend our money. Every new item that you bring home is another item that is taking up space in your surroundings. Try as you might convince yourself that material goods add joy to your life, they don't. There was an interesting experiment conducted to prove that notion too.

When a group of toddlers involved in the experiment only had four toys to play with, it was interesting to note that the toddlers were occupied for twice as long with just the four toys alone compared to when they had 16 toys around them to play with. The same can be seen in the way we live our lives. We may have 10 gadgets at home for example, but there are only one or two that get frequently used while the rest most likely only get brought out once in a while when there's a need for it, or never at all. That just goes to show that we have a lot of things in our homes that we don't actually need.

In another survey that was done, one-third of the participants involved admitted that they tried to avoid going home just to avoid dealing with the mess that they knew was waiting for them. Another survey discovered that about 90% of Americans believed that the clutter in their homes was negatively impacting their work and their lives. Eve more research revealed that Americans spent about *9 million hours per day* just looking for items at home that they misplaced. That's a lot of time to be spent looking for "lost" items. The stress that is caused by clutter is very real, and it's clear that something needs to change. There's a point when the clutter just gets to an unacceptable level, and that tipping point is when you no longer feel happy in your own home.

If you are embarrassed to have people over because you don't want them to see what a mess your home is, then you've got a problem. It's time to start reducing the mess to minimize the stress, and here's what you need to do to begin decluttering your home and your life:

- **Clear Out Your Room -** Your room is going to be the first thing you see in the morning when you wake up, and the last thing you see at night before you go to bed. What do you want to wake up and close your eyes to each day? A view that makes you sighs with contentment? Or a view that bothers you so much even when you're not looking at it, you're thinking about it throughout the day. You don't want your first thought every morning when you wake up to me *"I really need to clean this mess up"* because that's just going to throw off your entire mood and make it harder for you to start each day off on a positive note.

- **No More Impulsive Spending** - Each time you buy on impulse, remember this. *You're not in control of your decisions.* When you spend on a whim, you're acting on someone else's persuasion to get you to buy something you know deep down you don't need. Impulsive spending and purchases are the reason behind much of the clutter in your home. Put a stop to it, and you put a stop to clutter.

- **Unsubscribe from It All** - Get rid of all the emails that keep flooding your inbox for no good reason. If you don't even bother opening them and just straight away hit the delete button when you see them in your inbox, there's no good reason to keep them. Unnecessary emails are nothing more than a distraction, so hit the unsubscribe button and declutter them from your life.

- **No More Toxic People** - This form of decluttering is going to bring about one of the biggest changes in your life. Toxic people are no good for anyone, and the sooner you rid them from your life, the better off you will be. Toxic people are another form of distraction, and kind of negativity they emit is going to drain you of any energy you might have. Being exposed to this negativity long-term is one of the reasons you could end up with chronic stress. It's only when you declutter them from your life that you start to notice the difference.

- **Downsizing Your Social Media Accounts -** Social media is great for keeping in touch with the people you care about, but it's also where you get the most exposure to ads that lead you to make impulsive purchases you know that you don't need. The minute you log into any one of your social media accounts, you'll be faced with sponsored ad content. The only way to stay away from temptation is to remove it from your path entirely.

- **Organize Your Wardrobe -** It's more than likely that about the half the clothes that are in your closet right now haven't been used in more than six months. Yet, you keep buying more and trying to cram it into an already packed wardrobe and then feel stressed out when it's not going to fit. Having a closet crammed to its maximum capacity is not pleasant to look at, and if you want to minimize your stress, you need to start decluttering and getting rid of anything you no longer want or intend you wear ever again.

- **Decluttering Your Belongings -** Once you're done with your wardrobe, move onto your belongings. As you sort through your items, ask yourself how useful they are to you right now and when the last time you used it was. Do you intend to use it in the near future? Do you plan to ever use it at all? If it doesn't make sense to keep them around anymore, it's best to get rid of them. Your sanity will thank you for it.

- **Decluttering Your Gadgets -** Phones. Laptops. Tablets. You've probably accumulated a fair number of apps since you got those devices. Some apps you use daily, some you don't even remember downloading because you've forgotten about it entirely. Any apps that are no longer useful to you should be removed. It's going to have the same effect as spring cleaning your home. Spring cleaning your devices, keeping only a few necessary and essential apps on there is a lot easier on the eyes and your mind too. Your reduced stress levels will thank you for it when you can easily find what you need in less than a second.

- **Declutter Your Desk -** Piles of paperwork, files, stationery and random miscellaneous items on your desks can make it hard to get anything done. How do you even begin to focus on a task when you can't find what you need because it's buried in all mountains of paperwork and stuff that has piled up on your desk? Not to mention how disorganized it looks to your colleagues and superiors who happen to walk past your desk. Get an organized filing system in place and toss any papers and old documents that you no longer need.

Less Clutter, Less Fights

Clutter has the power to detail a relationship. Couples who live together are bound to eventually get into an argument over the mess around the house, and it's often the partner who has to do a lot of the tidying up that tends to get aggravated. Questions like: *Why do you need so much stuff? Why is your stuff everywhere? Why don't you ever put anything away? Do you really need to buy more books when you've got 50 books at home you never read?*

People are emotionally attached to their belongings, even if they won't admit it. That's why when one partner starts to question the other's need for so much stuff, that person becomes defensive. When both partners don't see eye to eye - one person prefers a neat and tidy environment, the other has a hard time getting rid of anything - there's going to be an inevitable clash of opinions.

But *why* does clutter have such enormous power that it can cause arguments, screaming battles and even the eventual breakup of a relationship when there's too much tension? It comes down to three reasons:

- Because of how our minds work.
- Because of the environment we live in.
- Because of the way we are perceived by others.

When one person is bothered more than the other by clutter, there's a problem. Based on a survey published in Consumer Reports

Magazine, couples were more than 40% more likely to fight about clutter and mess in the house. Our homes are like our territory, and when we feel our spaces are being invaded, we tend to become defensive, angry and even resentful towards the person we think is responsible for contributing to that mess, which is most of the time, our partner.

Some people might even feel too embarrassed about having friends over because of their partner's messy tendencies, believing that their home is not presentable enough and the thought of having people over stresses them out. Not feeling comfortable enough to invite friends over could mean that you might be missing out on opportunities to socialize, which might also make you resentful towards your partner and affect the relationship in the long-run. Your home needs to be a place so comfortable and inviting that even if you're not normally the sociable type, you still like the idea of being able to invite people over if you wanted to on the spur of the moment without having to worry about the state your house is in.

Clutter should never feel like it's more important than your relationship, and when one partner refuses to let go and get rid of the excess stuff that has accumulated, it can seem like the relationship doesn't matter enough to them to make that sacrifice.

Chapter 3:
Toss What You Don't Need

If your house always looks like it's been hit by a tornado and you never seem to be able to find what you're looking for, there's a problem. It's a problem when you become so used to living in a messy environment that you don't even think of it as a problem anymore. Because it is a problem. *A very big problem.* A messy, disorganized home is not just damaging to your mental and emotional health; it's hurting you physically too. The trouble is many of us don't realize that all those times we feel unhappy, stressed, tense, and we can't quite explain why it's because of the environment that we're surrounded in.

Around the home, there are a few designated areas which have a higher tendency to be more cluttered than others. These areas include:

- **The Kitchen -** It's a problem when the kitchen is messy because this is where all your food is prepared and stored. You're directly contributing to your poor physical health by allowing your kitchen to remain in a less than ideal state. The cross-contamination from the utensils, raw meat, and perhaps even un-sanitized kitchen countertops, for example, puts both you and your family at risk and vulnerable to food-borne diseases. Salmonella, E.coli, campylobacter and who knows what else are diseases which could seriously put you at risk of being hospitalized, and it's simply not worth it to put your health at risk that way. Not to mention all the pests which could be hiding away among all that clutter.

- **The Bathroom -** Another room that's a potential bacterial breeding ground, and a more serious potential health risk than the kitchen is your bathroom. Because of its environment, the bathroom is one of the few places where regular and frequent cleaning is needed, more so than any other room in the house to avoid mold, mildew, bacteria and all sorts of other parasites will be thriving in an environment that is not regularly cleaned and sanitized, even more, if its messy.

- **The Bedroom and Living Room -** Curtains that haven't been vacuumed or cleaned since you bought them, and bedroom and living room carpets that haven't been vacuumed regularly because there's too much stuff strewn all over the floor that it's too troublesome to pick up and move out of the way for regular cleaning is a problem. Again, you risk exposing yourself and anyone who is living with you to allergy-inducing elements like mold, dust mites and pet dander, not to mention all the other debris which might be floating around.

When your home starts to pose a danger to your health, it's clear that something needs to be done.

The Drawbacks of Having a Messy Home

Aside from the obvious embarrassment that others might think you're a slob, having a home that isn't neat and tidy does have its drawbacks, among which include:

- **Triggering Your Allergies** - No amount of medication or preventative measures are going to help you with your allergies if you don't deal with the root cause of the problem. A messy home. A cluttered home is a breeding ground for bacteria since we're less likely to clean it as often as we should when we don't want to be dealing with all that extra work of having to sort through our mess.

- **Unhappy Visitors** - Guests who don't feel comfortable coming to your home are not going to come back ever again. They'll be too polite to tell you it's because your house is too messy, but if you find that people keep turning down your invitations to come over to your place and hang out each time you invite them, there's probably a reason behind it. Nobody likes a messy house. No one. You may not notice your own mess after a while, but if you were to go over to someone's house and saw the messy environment they lived it, you wouldn't want to go back there again either. After a while, this is going to make you unhappy when you realize people are making excuses for staying away from you.

- **Mental Health Issues** - Anxiety caused by a messy environment could eventually lead to more serious mental health issues down the road. Like depression, for example. That's because it's impossible to feel genuinely happy and complete comfort in your environment if it isn't organized and neat enough. You don't have to be a neat freak or a perfectionist to enjoy the benefits of a clean and comfortable environment. Having a nice environment is something that we all want. Would you ever choose to live in a dingy, run-down apartment instead of a nice, comfortable, spacious home where sunlight streams through and fills the wide open spaces? No, you definitely wouldn't.

- **Accidents** - Living in a home packed in every corner and available surface space with stuff is an accident waiting to happen. When things are strewn about all over the place, there's a good chance you're going to trip up on one of these items one day and fall over. Hopefully, you don't end up falling down the stairs because that's going to hurt a lot, not to mention you run the risk of breaking something when you do or worse.

- **Obesity** - Would you believe if someone told you clutter could lead to obesity? Well, you better believe it. A study which was done back in 2017 by both Australia and the United States revealed there was a higher tendency to binge eats when you lived in a cluttered environment. Stress has been linked to overeating, and you're encouraging that habit the longer you continue to allow yourself to remain and live in clutter.

- **Poor Communication** - Cornell University's 2016 study highlighted that those who lived in clutter often found it difficult to relate to other people and understand their feelings. If you and your partner were living in a cluttered environment, the distraction from all the other stimuli that are being caused by the junk around your home is going to distract you enough that you can't concentrate on interpreting and understanding your partner's emotions. One of the reasons that clutter can cause a fight in relationships, further contributing to the levels of stress that you already feel.

Toss What You Don't Need

To find things around your home quickly, there's only one logical thing to do. Toss out everything else that you don't need and keep only the essentials. If you live in a home that is not as organized as it should be, on more than one occasion you would have found yourself turning your house upside down trying to find something you lost, wondering how on earth you managed to lose it in the first place. Here's the thing though, most of the time when you're searching for "lost" items around the house, and you're looking in the wrong place. Instead of searching the obvious, open areas, what you should be doing is looking in the most cluttered areas of your home. At least, that's what a study which was conducted by the University of Aberdeen concluded. Searching in the tidy areas is a futile and unproductive exercise. If it was there, you would have found it already because it would be hard to miss. Unless it was hidden behind a big pile of clutter.

- **Being in An Organized Home Saves You Time -** A disorganized home will cost you a lot more than just your sanity. When you spend a lot of time searching for items, you're wasting your time. You run late for appointments because you spent too much time searching for your keys. You're late for work and meetings because you couldn't find everything that you needed in one location. You pay your bills late because since there was no organized filing system for your bills and documents, you couldn't find what you were looking for and that caused a delay.

- **An Organized Home Brings Good Energy -** The ancient Chinese art of Feng Shui is rooted in the belief that when the elements of your home are aligned in an orderly, harmonious fashion, it aligns and enhances the vital energies in your life to bring you good fortune for happiness and prosperity. It's an interesting concept, and even if you don't necessarily believe in it, you can't deny that when your home is aligned in an aesthetically pleasing manner, it does make you feel good being in that kind of environment. You may not believe in good fortune or prosperity, but there's no disputing that a well-organized home is extremely beneficial, especially because it's hard to feel stressed when you're feeling good about where you live.

- **Keeping Track of Your Life -** Your stress can be significantly reduced when you can stay on top of all the appointments, errands, and tasks that you need to get done without feeling overwhelmed about it. Without organization, it's going to seem as if everything in your life is chaotic, even though the long list of things you have to do is actually more manageable than you think. Again, because you're feeling stressed about it, it becomes harder to think clearly and keep track of what you need to do with a clear head on your shoulders.

- **You Save Time Knowing Exactly What You Have -** When there's no unnecessary junk distracting and confusing you, it's easier to know exactly what resources you have in your home. When you need a pair of pants, you know just where to find them. When you need your outdoor sports equipment, you know just where they're kept. Need a specific book or magazine? You know where to go. With everything having a proper "home" in your home and stored away neatly in their designated storage spaces, life becomes a lot more efficient, and you'll rarely ever find yourself running late again when you're not scattered all over the place.

- **It Enhances Confidence -** An organized home by not be on your list of self-confidence enhancing techniques, but it should be. When you put in the time, discipline, and effort needed to keep your home neat and tidy; you feel good about yourself every time you look around and admire your handy work. The environment you created was entirely based on your hard work, and when you know you're capable of producing a result like that, it instills confidence within you that you can do anything you set your mind to. That sense of accomplishment becomes something you want to replicate repeatedly because of how good it makes you feel on the inside. Plus, there's a sense of pride that comes when other people start to admire and compliment you on how wonderful your home looks. It's an energizing feeling, and that takes your self-confidence levels up a notch.

- **You Respect Yourself -** Self-respect is another quality that everyone fosters within themselves. If you don't respect yourself first, it's going to be hard for others to respect you. Taking the time to put away your belongings neatly, treating these items with care is an exercise in self-respect. You worked hard to afford everything that you have in your home right now, and when you carelessly leave them all over the place where they're at risk of being damaged, you're not respecting the effort that went into working hard to afford your purchases.

- **It Encourages Self-Discipline -** It takes a lot more discipline than you realized to consistently keep your home neat and organized. When you take the time to put things away in its proper place, even when you're busy, it shows discipline and commitment on your part. Staying organized is a consistent effort, not a one-time thing, and making a commitment to doing this every day is an exercise in self-discipline. When you can show this kind of discipline in your home, you'll be able to transfer this dedication to other aspects of your life too.

Key Takeaway Points

Cleanliness is a reflection of who you are as a person. It's a habit that you cultivate and learn over time, and once you start to experience the difference it makes, there's no going back to what it used to be before. To sum it up, a cleaner, more organized environment eventually leads to a healthier, happier version of yourself, and here's why:

- You're more efficient when you know exactly where to find what you need at home.

- You're less stressed when you're not losing things around the home as often as you once were anymore.

- You spend less time looking for your things, which leaves you more time to handle more important tasks.

- You spend less money when you stop buying things that you don't need.

- Your home feels a lot of spacious and free when you don't have piles of the clutter taking up every available free corner.

- You feel a lot more peaceful and tranquil when your home is aesthetically pleasing.

- You look forward to coming home because you love being in an environment where you feel completely comfortable.

The benefits of having an organized household are something that you, your partner, and your family can enjoy together. It's a habit that is useful, especially if you've got young children living with you in your household. Teaching them the necessary organizational skills from the beginning is something they can benefit from for the rest of their life. Not only does it teach them a sense of responsibility, but it also makes them accountable for what they decide to surround themselves with. Whether their environment is one that infuses them with positive, productive energy is a choice that lies entirely with them, and it starts with learning how to organize their home and their life.

Chapter 4:
Your Organizational Rulebook

When you're new at anything, mistakes along the way are to be expected. This includes when you're about to reorganize your home and your life. Mistakes, however, are sometimes the best way for you to learn, so don't be too hard on yourself if it happens. The best way to minimize the mistakes that occur is to prepare beforehand by arming yourself with the knowledge about what these mistakes are so you can avoid them when the time comes.

Common Organizational and Decluttering Mistakes to Avoid

It's probably happened to you a few times in the past. You reached a point where you got tired of looking at the mess, decide to spring clean your entire home and went on a cleaning bender for several hours. You looked around at your home, feeling satisfied that it now looked much better, and then continued with your normal routine as life carried on. A few months later, your home is all messed up once again, and you're back to square one. It's exhausting, having to go through the same cycle, and cleaning for several hours is no easy task. Yet, the reason you find yourself back to where you started is that you continue to make the same mistakes unknowingly once you've organized your home.

How many of these common mistakes do you find yourself relating to?

- **Not Getting Rid of Bad Habits -** In order to change your lifestyle, your habits to change first. You can't aim to have a new, organized way of living if you still stick to your former bad habits. It'll just be cleaning out your clutter, only to accumulate a mess again and then have to clean once more. What you're trying to do now is break the cycle, which means ditching all those bad habits that led to a life of hoarding unnecessary items in the first place. Set rules to help you make decisions, and commit to them. Old ways may feel comfortable, but they may not be the most effective. Choose what you want to keep instead of what you want to get rid of. When you think about what you should keep instead, it helps you take on a more positive perspective and reduces the stress of being separated from your beloved things.

- **Pressure for Perfection -** Avoid putting pressure on yourself trying to be perfect. Decluttering is not about perfection, and if you are expecting it to be, you're only putting unnecessary pressure on yourself to achieve an unattainable concept. Decluttering your home and your life is not meant to be a process that is going to stress you out or something that you're going to regret later on. It shouldn't be a process that is forcing you to constantly think about how and what you could do better. Decluttering and organizing your home and your life is not about pursuing perfection; it is about pursuing happiness and balance in your life once again. Life is never perfect, and that is what makes a living each day so exciting, and the pressure for perfection is one mistake you need to avoid if you don't want the entire process to be unnecessarily stressful on yourself.

- **Being Too Hard on Yourself** - Being too hard on yourself during the decluttering process is a mistake that is going to make you miserable. It's your home and your life that you're decluttering, and the process can be what you want it to be. If you only want to declutter your living room, that's entirely up to you. If you're only comfortable decluttering your work station, again, that's a choice that's yours to make. It's about finding a balance that works for you, so you're more likely to stick to it, and there is certainly no rule that says you need to toss out almost everything that you own before you can consider the decluttering process successful. This lifestyle is going to be entirely personal and tailored to suit what works best for you, so you don't have to be too strict on yourself. If there's an aspect of the decluttering dynamic that that doesn't work well for you, you can choose to adapt and modify it into something that does work.

- **Using Decluttering as An Excuse to Buy More** - Another rookie mistake which often gets made is the idea that by decluttering the old stuff from our lives, we can buy new stuff because we now have more space. That is not what getting organized is about. You need to now learn to live with less and live with only what's important, that's the whole point. Decluttering is not a window of opportunity to go out and buy more new stuff just because you have all this extra space in your home. It is okay to have empty spaces around your home, not every area of your home needs to be crammed full of stuff.

- **Thinking That Decluttering Is an Automatic Path to Happiness -** Decluttering is not an automatic guarantee that you're going to be happy. You will be eventually, but maybe not in the way that you think. Getting rid of the clutter in your home and your life does not equal automatic happiness, and thinking that way will only lead to disappointment. The process doesn't work like that. Material possessions won't make you feel happy and fulfilled the way that you hoped, but neither will toss everything out. Happiness is something that comes from within, and it's not about how much or how little you have. It's more about teaching yourself to be *content* with what you have and to find happiness in the things that matter more than material goods. For true happiness to exist within you, you need to be happy with who you are and what you already have and to stop looking externally for a solution.

- **Trying To Stop Buying Anything At All -** This is bordering on extreme, and it's another classic mistake when trying to reorganize your home and your life. Stopping yourself from buying anything at all is impossible. If you genuinely have a need for something, you shouldn't restrict yourself from buying it. Shop less, but still shop and buy the things you only need to survive. Avoiding shopping altogether is almost impossible, but what you can do is find balance by changing the way that you now make purchases based on their priorities.

- **Believing That Decluttering Is Going to Fix Your Problems -** This is not a quick fix for happiness, and it is not a Band-Aid or magic formula that is going to make all your problems just go away. Undertaking this process with that kind of thinking, believing that it is going to help fix the problems you have in your life is only going to leave you feeling disappointed. The problems will still be there until you do something to fix it. Decluttering is meant to make life easier for you by removing the distractions, but it won't remove the problems, and doing it because that's the outcome you're hoping more means you're doing it for all the wrong reasons.

Rules to Living with Less

Even if you hate the mess that has gathered in your home, the idea of decluttering all the things you have accumulated over the years in your room sounds exhausting and overwhelming. Especially when you don't even know where to begin. As you look around what's your home, you might feel despair at the thought of how massive this decluttering project seems. It might take you hours, maybe even weeks before you can finally sort all of it out. But you've got to start somewhere and take it one step at a time to make the process more manageable.

Let's take a look at how you can start transforming your home into the organized heaven you didn't even know was possible:

- **Start It Out with A-List**: When you don't know where to begin, you begin by making a list. Write a list of the rooms around your home which you want to declutter, then look at the list again and start with the easiest one first and work your way up.

- **Have A Vision -** Try to envision what your life would be like when you apply this lifestyle and determine in your mind that this is really what you want to happen. Always start with the 'why.' Perhaps you intend to declutter to ensure you are able to focus on the important things in life. Perhaps, you are choosing this lifestyle to save money. Whatever it is, determining your 'why' is important because this is what you will fall back on every time you hit a roadblock.

- **One at A Time:** It is easy to feel overwhelmed when it looks like you have so much to do and not enough time to do it all. To make things easier, when you have finished decluttering one room in your home, what you need to do next is to stop. That's right. Stop and take a break, forget about decluttering for a while and go do some other activity. When you're ready and refreshed again, come back and work on the next room on your list. Repeat this process for each room.

- **Work at Your Own Pace**: It may be tempting to want to declutter and organize all the rooms in your home within a day, but let's be realistic. Work at your own pace and take your time; there is no reason to rush it. Slow and steady lets you do a much better, thorough job with each room.

- **Prepare Your Storage Spaces** – Prepare your storage spaces in advance before you start decluttering your room. That way, when you do begin, it'll be easier and quicker for you to sort items into their designated storage spaces, saving you a lot of time in the process.

- **Choosing the Right Container Sizes** - When most people think about packing away or storing their items, they think it's easier to just buy several big containers and dump everything in there to make the job easier. Unfortunately, this is the wrong way to go about it. What you should be doing instead, is first assessing the type of items you intend to store or organize, and then find the right container types for your items. Square containers, for example, are the best for holding a lot of items, while the clear, transparent containers offer the best visibility. If your items are stored away in clear containers, you'll still know exactly where to find what you need because you can see everything that's in there. Before going out and purchasing your containers, always measure the available space that you have and where you intend to keep those containers. The last thing you want is to buy something that doesn't fit. Don't forget to label your containers too, so you know what each box contains, even if you don't open the lid (unless they're clear containers, that is).

- **Keep Each Item Where They're Used the Most -** The flow around your home becomes a lot more efficient when you can easily find everything that you need because they're kept in the location they're being used the most. If you need a pair of scissors in every room in the house, go ahead and keep a pair in each room. Keep your notebook and pen right beside the phone where you know you're most likely going to be taking down messages. Keep another notebook and pen in the kitchen to make it easier to write your grocery list as you go. Keeping designed items in the areas where they're used the most makes your life much easier.

- **Treat Your Organized Spaces Like They Are Sacred -** Because they are. You worked hard to clear that space, why undo all that hard work and hours you put into achieving something good by going back to your old bad habits and just messing it up again? In your job, when you've done a fantastic job on a project or task that was assigned to you, you take pride in that, and you wouldn't do anything to jeopardize all that work you put into it. It's the same with the areas around your home that you worked hard to declutter. Treat your organized spaces like they're sacred, because they are, and put in the hard work now to keep the clutter away, so it never piles up again.

- **The 5-Minute Rule Daily** - Every day, make it a habit to give your home (and your workspace at the office), the 5-minute once over. Do a quick scan of every area in your room and see what needs to be tidied away and give yourself 5-minutes to do it. We can all spare 5-minutes out of the 24-hours in a day that we have to spend a little bit of time quickly clearing anything that might have gone astray in your hurry to get through the daily routine. Doing a little bit every day, even if it is for 5-minutes or less, prevents clutter from accumulating into an even bigger mess which might take hours to clear away because you procrastinated on it for far too long. A little bit every day goes a long, long way.

Decluttering and organizing can be a time-consuming process. But when you're done, and you step back and take a look at the way your home seems to have completely transformed, it will all be worth it.

Chapter 5:
Less Clutter & Greater Freedom

One of the first few things you need to do to maintain an organized, tidy home is to make a personal commitment to follow through and continue practicing this culture. Your commitment should start from this day forward. This commitment must include the rule that you cannot allow yourself to make excuses or justify why you're letting clutter accumulate in your home when you already know it serves no real benefit. Yes- it's going to be hard to do in the beginning, but the key here is to start small. It's the process, not the result. These small changes in your daily life will eventually lead to not just a more organized household, but an organized life in the long-run.

Freedom from Clutter: How to Maintain a Clutter-Free Home

If you want your home to stay organized, you need to learn to live with less and avoid holding onto the notion of being deprived. Because you're not "deprived" when you have everything that you need for your survival and to live comfortably enough. If you already have what you need, you will never be deprived. A lot of people are guilty of holding onto a lot of unnecessary items because of the all too common "just in case" or "what if I need it next time" fallacy, which is why they fear being "deprived" if they are without this item. If you haven't used it until this point, you're unlikely to need it anytime soon, which means that it is okay to be without this item and yes, you will survive either way.

Your mindset needs to be adaptable and not resistant to change. Only then can you transition from the person that you are right now, to the more organized person you want to be. Life is always going to be full of change, some of it good because you find it easy to cope, and some of it bad because you struggle to get through it. Change is inevitable, and if you're fixated on just one type of mindset, expecting everything else to conform according to what you think it should be, it's going to be a very difficult change for you to adapt and accept.

- **Do A Little Bit Every Day -** You don't have to clean out your home all in one go. It's okay to do a little bit every day as you slowly develop a habit and create an organizational routine for yourself that works.

- **Breaking It Down -** Have little decluttering goals for yourself, and then break down those goals into smaller, more actionable goals that are easier to stick to. For example, if your goal is to declutter your attic within a month, break it down into smaller goals which could include spending an hour or two over the weekend committed to cleaning it out a little bit at a time.

- **Don't Hold Onto the Past -** You must be willing to make the necessary changes which are needed if it means it is going to improve your life for the better. Not everyone has the willpower and the discipline to remove almost every material possession that they own in favor of a new way of living, *and* resist the temptation to give into making new purchases. Cutting things out of your life can be difficult, and you must be ready to let go of the past before you can move forward for a fresh start.

- **Don't Force Others to Follow Your Path -** This one is applicable if you're living with family or a partner under your roof. Although it is for the best, you have to remember that the decision to turn your household into a more organized one is a decision that you have made *for yourself.* You did not *have* to make this choice; you *chose* to do so instead. You can talk to your partner or your family about your new philosophy and approach to life, but don't expect them to conform and to be like you. It is up to them to live their lives the way that they want, even if you may not necessarily agree with it. Avoid forcing your ideas and your notions about what you think they should or shouldn't do because that's how you will end up alienating the people in your life.

- **Don't Give into Temptation -** It took a lot of effort for you to get to this point, and nothing about this process was probably easy for you. Every other person out there who made the decision to live a more organized life started off where you are today, having to make peace with the knowledge that they will now have to resist all their old temptations and be disciplined so that they don't revert back to their old ways and unhealthy habits. You must now train yourself to be disciplined enough to only buy what they need to keep the clutter from once again accumulating in your home.

- **The Difference between Want and Need -** To avoid clutter from coming back over and over again, you must learn to distinguish between needs and wants. When an urge pops up, stop, and ask yourself, *do I really need this? Or do I just want it?* Not every urge is going to be a need, and that is something that you will need to learn to distinguish over time. It takes time to finally be able to separate desires from necessities.

- **Quit Making Stuff A Priority -** Relationships, people you love and care about, and life experience will always mean more than items ever will. No item will ever be able to fill the lonely void you may experience without meaningful relationships in your life, and no item will ever be able to bring you the kind of lasting, meaningful happiness that you seek. Which is why when you choose embarked on this journey, to begin with, you must come to terms with the fact that making items a priority will never be the right path to take. Avoid forming personal attachments to your belongings, because will only make it much harder to get rid of, and the desire to want more will never truly leave you if you still believe material possessions are going to be the most important thing in your life.

- **Look After Your Items -** Since you're now going to have fewer possessions, start looking after each item carefully and treasure everything that you have. Caring for your possessions reduces the need to keep buying new items because again, you're already happy and grateful with what you have. Looking after your items happen almost instinctively without even having to think much about it when you're consciously grateful.

- **Regular Purging -** Decluttering is not just a one-time process. It's a habit, and to keep your home clutter free long-term, you need to carry out regular reviews and purges of your belongings, just to make sure that the clutter is not piling up again without you realizing. You could do this every couple of months, maybe even twice in a year, but you're going to need to purge regularly and comb through your inventory of belongings. Anything that hasn't been used in a while must go. Anything that does not serve a practical or functional purpose must go. Clothes that you kept during the first round of the decluttering process, but then realized you haven't worn or touched yet must go. Go through their belongings every now and then, and eliminate everything that is not necessary. This is how you maintain that organized home and lifestyle and make it a part of your routine.

Organizing Tips to Make Life Easy

The rules of decluttering may be arbitrary, but there are certain dos and don'ts that you can abide by to help you sustain and successfully maintain this lifestyle.

- **Don't Store It, Toss It -** Reorganizing your space, your life and all the little details that wear your down means that in a few months' time, you'd be rearranging again. Instead of doing that, toss things out. Toss, don't keep, because you're not getting rid of the clutter when you do that. The clutter is still going to be there, even if you put it out of sight. If you have not used it for the past six months to 1 year, time to say goodbye.

- **No More Shopping During Sales -** Going shopping during a sale only means you'd end up bringing home more stuff, and that's not what decluttering is supposed to be about. Just because it's cute and it's on sale doesn't mean you should get it. Unless it's absolutely essential to your survival, you can live without it.

- **Starting Out Small -** The easiest way to begin the decluttering process and be able to see it all the way through is to start small. Instead of purging out and declutter everything in one weekend, try opening a drawer or a cabinet, get a box and de-clutter.

- **Learn to Be Grateful With What You Already Have -** Being happy with what you already have reduces the need to keep buying more, or looking for the next new thing that you think is going to make you happy. When you're no longer buying the essentials during your shopping trips, it probably means you already have everything that you need to survive happily. You just don't realize it because you're not consciously reminding yourself to be grateful for everything that you already have.

- **Don't Buy It Unless You're Replacing It -** Instead of making a new purchase, start getting into the habit of only buying new items if your current ones need to be replaced. Adding on new items without tossing out any of the old ones is only going to add to the clutter in your home. If something new is coming in, something old needs to go out to create a balance. You don't need two items of everything in your home.

- **Remember That Less Is More -** If you like uncomplicated stuff, clean surfaces, organized things, then furnishing your home with just the essentials is more than enough to make you happy. It's okay if not every corner or surface is filled with something. Sometimes, having empty spaces might be just what you need.

- **If You Can Borrow It, Do It -** If there's an item you need, but you know you're only going to use it once, considering borrowing instead of buying. This includes items of clothing. There are plenty of online fashion outlets that specialize in borrowing items on a certain fee.

- **If You Can Fix It, Do It -** Instead of immediately tossing out an item or piece of clothing if it's broken or torn, see if it can still be fixed before you give up on it entirely. Choose to fix their items instead of immediately resorting to making new purchases. Focus on buying items which are durable. Not only is it going to last you a lot longer, but the possibility of repairing it is also often successful, saving you a lot of money in the process and valuable time when you don't have to shop around for a suitable replacement.

- **Being Mindful Of Your Purchases -** No more buying on a whim, those days are going to have to be put behind you now. Oh, you will still need to shop, but you are going to do differently from now on is to practice *mindful shopping*. This means that you're going to now think long and hard about each item before you purchase it, weighing the pros and cons and whether these items are necessary or essential. You need to factor in the functionality and practicality of each item, and in what way it is going to enhance your life. It sounds like a lot of work to do before making any purchase, but once you get used to the process, you'll be able to go through the motions without even really thinking about it.

- **Go Digital -** Where possible, consider minimizing your paper trail by taking documents like your finances, paperwork, billing, data keeping, and so on in your computer or cloud drives. Scan your documents, scan your photos and place them all in your cloud drive- you'd find that it is a lot more secure and safer, and the added benefit is, it doesn't take up any extra space in your home.

The freedom that you get by living with less can be a lot more liberating than you may think. It's not just about downsizing all your belongings for the sake of clearing away the mess in your home alone. No, it is much more than that. It is about clearing your entire life and redefining it to have more purpose and meaning than it once did before. The general rule is that for something to become a habit, you need to stick to the routine for about 21-days or so. The initial 21-days is when you're going to have to put in most of the hard work into the process and to be disciplined and not give up halfway through when the going gets tough. Stick it out for this first couple of days and being an organized person will eventually become a habit that is ingrained and a part of your life. You will be amazed at how this experience can bring you a sense of peace, not just in your home, but in every other aspect of your life too.

Conclusion

Thank for making it through to the end of this book, let's hope it was informative and able to provide you with all of the tools you need to achieve your goals whatever they may be.

Japanese organizing consultant Marie Kondo summed it up perfectly when she called the decluttering and organizing process *"life-changing magic."* You don't quite realize what a difference a neat and tidy home can do for your health and mental wellbeing until you begin mindfully observing how you felt before and after the decluttering process.

We need to spend more time thinking about the way our environment affects us. Emotions can be a very powerful element, not something that should be taken lightly at all. How you feel affects your life on many levels, and high levels of stress over a long period can be detrimental to your health. It simply isn't worth it to be miserable when you could do something to make a difference. To take charge of your life and happiness once again, and it all begins with a simple decision to simply keep your home, and your life organized.

Finally, if you found this book useful in any way, a review on Amazon is always appreciated!

Description

Toss what you don't need. That's what you need to do to be happy.

Contrary to popular belief, your happiness *DOES NOT* hinge on how much you own. How much you own is actually making you *unhappy* when your home can no longer accommodate all your stuff. What should be a warm, cozy, comfortable sanctuary then turns into a cluttered nightmare as you start to feel suffocated by your belongings and yearn for an escape.

That escape comes from organizing your home. Organize your home and everything else in your life will fall into place. Organize your home and watch yourself sail through your tasks more efficiently than ever before. Organize your home and say goodbye to all that time you used to waste searching your "misplaced" or "lost" items that took up way more time than it should.

Think it's only your job that's causing you stress. Think again. *Your home* could be the secret stress trigger you least expected. The environment you spend a lot of your time in is the one that is going to affect you the most, and other than your office, that's going to be your home.

Organized Home: Declutter and Organize Your Home and Life is going to walk you through what you need to take your home from messy to classy, as you learn to:

- The rules of living with less
- How a messy home could be holding you back
- Why less clutter can lead to greater freedom
- Why a happy home is a tidy home
- How to keep your home organized and clutter free long-term

Tired of feeling stressed out by the mess in your home? Then it's time to do something about it once and for all.

Home Cleaning Tips:

Introduction

Congratulations on purchasing your copy of *Home Cleaning Tips*. Thank you for doing so. As a 35-year old woman with a toddler, I know how difficult it can be to attempt to keep a home clean when you have constant activities. It is vital to keep a home as germ-free as possible to ensure the safety of your youngster as well as you and everyone else in your home.

This set of guidelines will help you begin the process from the floor to the ceiling (literally) using natural cleaning products. Of course, you will need to supply the 'elbow grease' to get it accomplished. I have a passion for cleanliness in which I would love to share with you to also save a huge chunk of time and money.

If you need to stick to a budget, you are in the right place. The first segment will provide you with general cleaning supplies and how to prepare them. The following chapters will provide you with a thorough room-to-room method of cleaning. You will have new ideas suggested throughout your book with new ways to clean your home.

Let's get started and get down to the basics of cleaning your space for your baby!

First, one humorous note observed by a parent (boasting of course.) One mom said her child only eats organic foods. The second parent said, "Good for you. My kids eat Fritos off the floor!" Is your floor that clean or safe?

Chapter 1:
Go with Natural Cleaning Products

To keep a tidy home for your youngster; you need to have the essential cleaning products to get the job done. To help get you started, I have provided you with a general batch of supplies you will need to clean each of your living spaces.

Essential Homemade Cleaning Containers

Before you get started, it is essential to store all of your cleaning products securely, just in case your toddler is successful in opening or finding an open cabinet. These are just a few of the items you will need:

- *Plastic Containers with Lids:* Ziploc-type containers are an excellent choice with its secure lid. Just make the chosen cleaner mixture is clearly marked for future use. Some products will have a shelf life.

- *Spray bottle or two (glass is preferred)*: You will be mixing many chemicals that may need different types of containers. It is best to purchase high-quality containers, but if you're on a budget, Dollar General will have one or two to choose from in stock.

- *Shaker Containers*: Choose a container with a tight-fitting lid when possible. Save a parmesan cheese container or make your own using another option of choice.

- *Buckets:* If you need to do more than a spot clean, you will need a bucket or two. If you use a mop, a mop bucket would be needed. Otherwise, a smaller bucket will come in handy for cleaning other areas such as baseboards. You must be diligent with a toddler lurking. If you have a toddler, chances are you would like to remain within your spending range for household cleaners. These are a few of the basics for frugal cleaning:

Natural Cleaning Products

Baking Soda: Toss the Comet and Ajax aside by using a portion of baking soda. It is good from scrubbing the toilet, to the sparkling carpet, and everything in between. It is also a great deodorizer and natural air freshener.

White Vinegar: You will achieve a natural disinfectant which is safely mixed using a one-to-one ratio with water. Use it to clean the cabinets, countertops, and floors as a great grease cutter. It's awesome for cleaning stainless fixtures. Spray the mixture onto your rugs or carpets. If you don't like the smell of it, just open the windows for the air to clear. Instead of purchasing an expensive product for the dishwasher such as Jet Dry, add a little vinegar into the cycle. Consider adding it to your laundry cycle in the place of regular fabric softener.

Hydrogen Peroxide: Add a sprayer nozzle to a bottle of peroxide since the elements can break down when exposed to sunlight. Use a one-to-one ratio of water and peroxide if you want it diluted further. Spray down all of the countertops in the bath and kitchen areas to kill germs. You can also use hydrogen peroxide to remove stains including juice, blueberries or other berries, and blood.

Liquid Castile Soap: If you find vinegar offensive, use this soap as a great multipurpose cleaner. Use it as a personal care product and cleaning. Add a bit of water and tea tree oil for another multipurpose cleaner.

Natural Dish Soap: Not only will the soap cut through grease on your dishes, but you can also add it to a spray bottle and clean your kitchen surfaces. Have one in the bath and kitchen. It is also great for laundry stains.

Borax: Borax is made of Boron which is an essential mineral the body actually needs to function correctly but, just like with most things, in excess, it can be harmful. Is it safe? You <u>can</u> decide.

Microfiber Cloths: Purchase one of these cleaning cloths to clean your entire house (not the toilet). All you need is water to clean the surface. Choose a different color for each of your areas, so you don't cross contaminate.

Microfiber Cloth Mops: You can also purchase a chemical-free version of microfiber for a cleaning option using just water.

Sponges: You probably already have a stash of odor-free sponges that will work great with your new natural-cleaning products. You will also benefit with a Magic Eraser, a melamine sponge. It is best used by adding water first. If that doesn't remove the stubborn mark or dirt, just dip it in a little soapy water. You can also use your all-purpose cleaner with a little peppermint or lemon oil on a sponge mixed with warm water. Be sure to test a space before using the Magic Eraser to ensure it is safe.

Scrub Brushes: It's important to designate separate scrub brushes for particular jobs to avoid any cross-contamination. You can use a small toothbrush for small spaces such as around spigots (of course, a new one).

Squeegee: A squeegee will change the way you look at window cleaning. All you need to do is spray the chosen window cleaner on the window and away goes the grime. You can also purchase one that has a sponge attached if your outside windows are particularly dirty. Just dip the sponge in the cleaner bucket, scrub the window, and squeegee away the grime. You will need a couple of towels in the workspace to avoid spills or drips.

Broom & Mop: You will need the old-fashioned team, but just for quick clean-ups or spills. You can choose different types of mops including a twistable mob, sponge mop or my favorite, a refillable mop with microfiber pads. Just throw the pads in the washer for a sanitary clean the next time it's needed.

Dusting Wands: The best dusting wand to choose is one with a removable, washable duster. It should be capable of reaching the tall ceilings and corners with ease.

Vacuum Cleaner with Attachments: Select a high-quality vacuum that is within your budget. Be sure it has a good warranty. All you need to do is empty and clean the canister, or replace the bag often for the best results.

Lastly, if your budget allows, a wet/dry vacuum could save you a ton of stress.

You will also use many other items including:

- Lemons
- Natural salt
- Oven cleaner (see recipe)
- Bleach
- Wood polish (see recipe)
- Glass Cleaner (see recipe)
- An all-purpose cleaner (see recipe)

- Kitchen cleaner or wipes
- Rubber gloves
- Paper towels and cleaning cloths
- Toilet Brush
- Funnel

Essential Oils: (Optional) These are a few of the most popular scents to add to your cleaning products. Essential oils provide many benefits, but for now, the focus is on disinfecting and cleaning qualities. Be sure you purchase essential oils - not fragrance oils. However, the list is unlimited:

- Tea Tree Oil: Antifungal, antibacterial, antiviral, antiseptic, & antimicrobial
- Eucalyptus: Deodorizer & anti-infective
- Lemon: Antiviral, anti-infective, antiseptic, & antifungal
- Lime: Air Freshener
- Grapefruit: antiseptic & air freshener
- Clove: Air freshener
- Orange: Air freshener
- Lavender: Antifungal, anti-infective, & antiseptic

- Peppermint: Antiviral, antiseptic, antifungal, & Antibacterial

- Rosemary: Antiviral, antiseptic, antimicrobial, antifungal, & antibacterial

Caddies or Tool Containers: You will need to corral your tools and cleaners in a caddy that will easily fit in a closet or pantry that is out of reach of your children. Store them in spaces where the most clean-up is needed.

Now it is time to add a more extensive explanation of how to clean and maintain your living space, so your toddler is ensured to enjoy clean surfaces all over the house from top to bottom!

Clean the Couches & Chairs

If you aren't sure of the fabric of your couch the manufacturer should have a label somewhere indiscreetly sewn into the seam of the fabric. Check underneath the cushions or the base of the furniture. You should see a label with some of the following descriptions:

- *SW:* Water or Solvent cleaner is safe to use.

- *W:* Okay to use water for cleaning.

- *S:* Use only solvent-based cleaners.

- *X:* Use Only the Vacuum for cleaning.

Once you have decided how to proceed with the type of cleaner, use this process to clean the soiled couch or chair.

- *Step 1:* Use a brush or white cleaning rag to groom the entire space to help remove any dried-on spots of food or other debris.

- *Step 2:* Sprinkle a large amount of baking soda over the entire couch. The soda will help to absorb any nasty smells and helps break up any stains lingering in the fabric.

- Wait for 20 minutes to an hour before you use the brush attachment of your vacuum cleaner to sweep away the powder.

- *Step 3:* Clean the sofa with the below cleaner if needed.

    Cleaning Tip: Be sure to test an unnoticeable spot before you spray the entire sofa.

Cleaner for Fabric Furniture:

What You Need:

- White Vinegar (1 tablespoon)

- Dish Washing Liquid (1 teaspoon)

- Warm Water (1 cup)

- Baking Soda (1 teaspoon)

How to Clean:

Baking soda is the base and vinegar is the acid that creates carbon dioxide. The results are lots of cleaning bubbles.

- Add the dish liquid into a spray bottle with the vinegar.

- Pour in the warm water.

- Combine the mixture over the sink. Add the baking soda, and quickly screw on the top of the sprayer.

- Use the mixture to clean the entire surface of the couch.

- Be sure it is thoroughly dry before you place any items directly on its surface.

Other Natural Cleaners for The House

The cleaners in this segment are basics you will use throughout your home to keep it bacteria-free (as much as possible with a busy youngster).

Lemon & Clove Liquid Dish Soap

Lemon and clove are fresh scents to include in your kitchen tools. The combination will make your dishes streak-free and sparkling clean.

What You Need:

- Lemon essential oil (10-15 drops)
- Citrus castile soap/unscented castile soap (8 oz.)
- Clove essential oil (5 drops)

Variations of What You Need:

- *Citrus:* Substitute lime, orange, or grapefruit for the clove.
- *Grease Fighter:* Add a splash of white vinegar to the warm dishwater.

How to Prepare:

- Pour the soap and oils into a storage container and shake well.
- *To Use:* Add 1-2 squirts to the dishwater and scrub away.
- *To Store:* Store on the counter or safely away from your toddler's reach.

Lemon Dishwasher Powder - Detergent

You want to be sure the foods you serve your youngster is served on clean and sanitized dishes. You will get that with these amazing non-toxic chemicals.

Yields: 24 loads @ 1 heaping tbsp. per load

What You Need:

- Baking soda (1 cup)
- Arm & Hammer Super Washing Soda (1 cup)
- Borax (1 cup)
- Lemon essential oil (20 drops)

Variations of What You Need:

- *Unscented Product*: Leave out the essential oil
- *For Hard Water*: Add a ½ cup portion of Epsom salts.
- *Citrus Aroma*: Add 10 drops each of lemon and orange essential oils.
- *Peppermint & Lemon*: Use 10 drops of each oil.

How to Prepare:

- Combine the components in a large mixing bowl.
- *To Use:* Put one heaping tablespoon per load in the dish detergent compartment. Run as usual.
- *To Store*: Pour the mixture into a glass bottle or other container with a lid. Dress it up with an antique colored canning jar. It will keep the mixture dry until it's needed.

Disinfectant Wipes:

What You Need:

- Wide-Mouth mason jar (1-quart size or 4-6 cup capacity & tight-fitting lid)
- Cleaning cloths - 10x10 squares (15-20)
- Filtered water (.75 cup)
- White distilled vinegar (.75 cup)
- Lemon essential oil (15 drops)
- Lavender essential oil (8 drops)
- Bergamot essential oil (4 drops)

How to Prepare:

- Combine all of the fixings in a mason jar or other type of glass storage container. Note; the essential oils could have an adverse effect on plastic.
- Swirl the components to combine.
- Push the rags into the solution to soak. Securely close the lid and rotate the jar as needed to keep the rags moist.
- Use any time for a quick clean up, so your toddler has a clean place for his/her precious cargo.

All-Purpose Cleaner:

- Fill a 32-ounce spray bottle up to an inch or two below the fill line. Leave room to add the soap and essential oil.

- Add approximately 2 tablespoons of castile soap (peppermint, citrus or any scent you like or even unscented).

- Add 10 to 20 drops of tea tree oil.

- Shake gently to combine.

- This cleaner can be used anywhere you would use a vinegar cleaner or any other conventional multipurpose cleaner around your house.

Glass Cleaner:

This fabulous cleaner is great to have around for all those cute little fingerprints!

What You Need:

- Water (2 cups - filtered or distilled)

- Essential oil of choice (10 drops)

- Vinegar (2 tbsp.

- Spray bottle (glass is preferred)

- Microfiber cloth

How to Clean:

- Combine each of the fixings into the spray bottle.
- Spray on your windows or any other glass surface using the fragrance of your choice; many use lemons.

Vinegar Clean-Up in A Bottle:

If you prefer a spray bottle; all you need is a solution of three parts of water to one part of vinegar. Use it for any cleaning job from shining windows to the garbage disposal.

Cleaning Tip Warning: Don't use vinegar on colored fixtures or brass; it might cause discoloration.

Lemon Household Cleaner

What You Need:

- Water (8 oz.)
- Distilled white vinegar (4 oz.)
- Tea Tree Oil (15 drops)
- Lemon essential oil (15 drops)
- Glass - cleaning spray bottle

How to Use:

- Fill the bottle with all ingredients and mix.
- Shake the contents before each cleaning job.

Tip: It is advisable to use a glass container when possible. The citrus essential oils are highly concentrated and have acidic properties. Sometimes, it is best to store the products in glass for this reason.

Lemon Juice for Stubborn Stains:

If you have a stubborn sink stain; try this remedy:

What You Need:

- Powdered Borax (½ Cup)
- Lemon Juice (juiced - ½ of 1)

How to Clean:

- Use a sponge to dab the mixture, rub, and rinse with hot water.
- The method works well on stainless steel, porcelain, enamel, and many others.

Scouring Powder:

What You Need:

- Salt - not iodized (.5 cup)

- Washing soda (.5 cup) Ex. Arm & Hammer

- Baking soda (1 cup)

- Optional: Lemon essential oil (5 drops)

How to Clean:

- Pour the components into a bowl or jar.

- Mix well and store in a shaker.

- If you do not have a shaker, use a jelly jar and punch holes in the top.

- Clean using the concoction whenever you have a stubborn stain.

Tip: For tougher surfaces, apply undiluted white vinegar and water to the surface. Sprinkle the powder on the surface to sit for about five minutes.

Scrub with a sturdy brush and rinse with more vinegar and water.

Soft Abrasive Cleaners:

If you prefer using a product such as Soft Scrub to clean your porcelain sinks or similar spaces, you can use a natural source without using bleach.

How to Clean:

- Get the sink wet.

- Sprinkle a portion of baking soda on the surfaces.

- Use a cleaning rag to clean the surface until the sink or other surface is sparkling.

Vinegar for Limescale:

The white spots in your sink are lime deposits from mineral-rich hard water. Try this formula to clean the surfaces:

- Soak a paper towel with vinegar.

- Wrap the towel around the spotted area.

- Wait for ten minutes.

- Buff dry with a paper towel.

Natural Toilet Bowl Scrubber

What You Need:

- Vinegar (1 cup)
- Borax (.75 cup)
- Tea Tree essential oil (.5 tsp.)
- Lemon essential oil (5 drops)

How to Use:

- Combine all of the ingredients in a medium glass container.
- Measure the portions (¼-½ cup) in the toilet bowl. Let it sit for several minutes.
- Use a brush to remove the stains.

For a Spray: You can also make it a bit thinner to use as a spray.

For a Scrub: Add a ¼ cup portion of baking soda to the mix and use gloves to scrub the toilet.

Homemade Drain Cleaner:

You don't need to purchase a bunch of fancy cleaning products for maintaining a clean and clear drain. Use one of these simple solutions:

Product 1: Clear the Drain

What You Need:

- Baking Soda (.75 cup to 1 cup)

- Vinegar (.5 cup)

How to Clean:

- Pour the baking soda in the drain.

- Pour the vinegar into the drain and immediately cover the drain.

- Leave everything to sit and work for about 30 minutes, but don't use the sink during this time.

- After 30 mins, run hot water run thru the pipes for about 2 to 3 mins.

- For really tough clogs you may need to repeat, but if you do this on a regular basis (about once a month) it keeps my drains clear and fresh without any problems.

Product 2: Drain Freshener

What You Need:

- Baking Soda (1 Cup)

- Cream of Tartar (¼ Cup)

- Salt (1 Cup)

How to Clean:

- Make a habit of pouring one-half cup of the mixture down the drain.

- Pour a quart of boiling water in after you have added the mixture.

- Do this every few weeks.

Clear Away Rust Spots:

- Use a bit of lighter fluid or WD-40 on the spot and rinse it completely.

- For porcelain, pour salt on ½ of a lemon a rub the area until it is shiny clean.

Natural Wood Cleaner

You don't want to take any chances with your table when cleaning it. This sounds almost good enough to eat:

- Squeeze juice of one lemon into a small jar.

- Pour in 1 tablespoon of olive oil.

- Measure and pour in 1 tablespoon of water.

- Shake thoroughly until it emulsifies.

- Pour a small amount on a soft cloth and clean all of the wood furniture. This is also excellent if you have wood paneled rooms.

Dusting Spray for Cleaning Furniture:

This is a fabulous choice to bring the luster back to your furniture. However, this mixture shouldn't be used on glass, walls, granite, or stainless steel since it contains oil. Avoid using it on fine antiques or unfinished wood.

What You Need:

- Vinegar (.5 cup)
- Water (1 cup)
- Oil of choice (2 tbsp.) ex. grapeseed, sunflower, or olive
- Cedarwood essential oil (5 drops)
- Lemon essential oil (10 drops)
- Brown amber bottle

How to Clean:

- Pour the vinegar and water into a spray bottle.
- Add in the oils and shake.
- Cover the bottle and store.

- Tip: A brown bottle is suggested since the essential oils are potent and could damage a plastic bottle over long periods of time.

Carpet Cleaning

Use preventive maintenance to eliminate part of the dirt that can enter your home and become embedded into your carpet. Begin by arranging doormats in front of each of your home's entrances. Vacuum your carpeting at least twice each week to ensure your youngster cannot pick up any undesirable morsels. You also help control dust, dust mites, and other irritants. Invest in a strong vacuum with a HEPA filter.

Nontoxic Alternatives:

For baby-safe carpet cleaning, use non-toxic, non-irritating alternatives to chemical cleaners. Be sure to soak up liquid spills immediately by gently blotting with an absorbent cloth or a paper towel. Don't rub. Try one of these solutions:

- Sprinkle baking soda, cornstarch or cornmeal over greasy stains.

- Plain club soda removes some stains including red wine.

- Help remove any sticky 'stuff' using a piece of ice. Scrape off hard substances with using a butter knife, then mix 1/2 teaspoon liquid dish detergent with 1 cup warm water or mix

2/3 cup warm water with 1/3 cup white vinegar. Spray with the solution. Clean the spot.

- Steam cleaning with plain water or, for stubborn stains, 2 1/2 gallons of water mixed with 1 1/2 cups of white vinegar is another effective option.

Avoid the area and steer the toddler to another area for about six hours. Carpets that don't dry efficiently are prone to mold, mildew, and fungal growth. When wetting your carpet, open the windows for fresh air circulation. Vacuum the spot. Baking soda also makes an ideal deodorizing agent.

To keep your carpet completely baby-safe, unless it's an emergency, don't wet-wash a carpet on humid days. Use fans, pointing them directly them over damp carpeting. Choose products you know will be safe for your toddler such as the ones described in this cleaning book of guidelines. After the carpet dries, just sprinkle with baking soda and wait a few minutes for it to absorb the odors. Vacuum as usual.

Carpet Freshener

What You Need:

- Cinnamon Leaf essential oil (30 drops)

- Lemongrass essential oil (30 drops)

- Clove Bud essential oil (10 drops)

- Eucalyptus essential oil (30 drops)

- Bicarbonate soda/Baking soda (.5 cup)

How to Prepare & Use:

- Simply blend all of the ingredients in a wide mouth jar.

- Close the lid for 24 hours.

- Add a sprinkle when the carpet needs refreshing, and leave it for 10 to 15 minutes before you vacuum away the residue.

Chapter 2:
Cleaning Kitchen Spaces

If you have a toddler and you think your kitchen is clean, all you need to do is turn around a few times, and your baby has probably found a way to find a new distraction causing another messy cleanup.

Let's take a look at the kitchen cleaning methods and clean from the countertops to the kitchen floor.

The Kitchen Sink:

It's time to tackle the kitchen sink. Just because you wash out the sink daily after you do a load of dishes, doesn't mean it is clean. Water spots, rust, soap scum, and food stains can build up if you don't stay ahead of them.

Porcelain Sinks: If you have a porcelain sink, you can make it gleam with this process:

- Line the sink with paper towels.
- Soak them with bleach.
- Let them soak for 30 minutes, and discard them.
- Rinse the sink with hot running water.

Note: Don't use bleach on colored porcelain because it will fade. Instead, use vinegar, baking soda, or a mild detergent (and a bit of elbow grease).

Now that you have the sink clean, you can protect it from scratches and stains by installing a plastic mat on the bottom of the sink. The mat will protect the shiny sink from lingering acidic foods/liquids such as salad dressing, vinegar, and fruit.

The Garbage Disposal: If you smell something that seems rancid, it could be the garbage disposal needs some cleaning also. Simply, grind a few lemons in the unit to make it fresh and clean. Repeat the process every few weeks. You can also sprinkle baking soda in the drain for several hours before running the disposal. For a deeper clean, use this method for the garbage disposal drain:

What You Need:

- White Vinegar (1 Cup)
- Baking Soda (.5 cup)

How to Clean:

- The mixture will fizz (remember pop rocks candy from the 1970s) with a popping noise.
- Wait a few minutes.
- Pour boiling water down the drain.

- Fill the drain with 2 cups of ice.

- Pour one cup of salt in the drain over the ice cubes (rock salt or sea salt is a good choice if you have it).

- Turn the cold-water faucet to the on position.

- Turn on the disposal unit.

- Run the disposal until the ice is gone.

- The grime and debris should be loosened. Cut a lime or lemon in half and let the disposal chew them up for a deodorized drain.

Sanitizing the Sponges

Did you ever ask the question, "is that a clean sponge"? You can sanitize your sponge by tossing it into the microwave for ten to twenty seconds. It will kill all of the bacterial germs hiding in the nooks and crannies! Let them air dry thoroughly. Make an attempt to replace them every two weeks.

Clean Small Appliances

- ***Toasters:*** Remove the crumbs from the toaster and toaster oven. Clean the racks with hot, soapy water to remove any food debris.

- *Can Opener:* Take the opener apart and clean the cutter by soaking it in hot, soapy water. Scrub the blade with a scouring pad if necessary. Be careful, so you don't get cut on the sharp blade.

- *The Blender:* If you have ever tried to clean a blender, you know how involved the process can become. Simply add some soapy water in the blender, blend, rinse, and dry — no more hands on the sharp blades, or first aid kits necessary for the job.

- Wipe all surfaces of the other small appliances.

Clean the Microwave

Remove any trays and wash them in hot, soapy water. Use an all-purpose cleaner to wipe and scrub the entire unit. Be sure to spray the cleaner on the rag or sponge; not directly in the microwave.

You can also go the natural route with a few sliced lemons and a bowl of water in the microwave. Turn the unit on high until the microwave is steamy. Let it steep for a few minutes to cut through the grease and grime. You can easily wipe out the moisture, and replace it with a fresh smelling space.

Clean the Refrigerator

Begin at the top of the refrigerator and remove everything. Clean out each shelf as you proceed. If any of the drawers or shelves are removable, take each unit out, and use warm soapy water to clean it. You want to clean every surface, especially the ones on the door—inside and out.

Before placing your food back inside of the fridge, line the shelves with some parchment paper or plastic food wrap to make cleaning a breeze. If you have a small mess, just remove the layer of plastic, and it is clean!

Super-Clean the Oven

Use natural products to clean the oven manually. You can choose from several techniques for general cleaning of your oven.

Natural Oven Cleaner: Option 1: Simply apply a layer of baking soda and spray it with a vinegar solution. It should form a paste. Leave the mixture on the surface of the oven for five minutes. Wipe the oven with a damp rag or sponge.

Natural Oven Cleaner: Option 2: First, take a look at one of the general natural cleaning options using baking soda:

What You Need:

- Baking soda

- Water
- Spray bottle

How to Clean:

- Begin by spraying the oven with water, so it's damp.
- Sprinkle a ¼-inch layer of the soda, making sure you cover the entire surface.
- If you see a dry spot, respray it with the water.
- Let the mixture rest for at least three to four hours with the oven *OFF*.
- Wipe the paste with an old towel to remove the grime.
- It could take several applications, but thank goodness, it is natural.

Natural Oven Cleaner: Option 3: If you're in a hurry, this will help remove the stuck-on grease and food.

What You Need:

- Baking soda (3 tbsp.)
- Warm water (1 cup)
- Castile soap (1 tbsp.)

Variations:

- Lemon & Clove: Add 5 drops each.

- Lemon: Add 10 drops essential oil

- Lemon & Rosemary: Add 5 drops of each oil.

How to Clean:

- Add all of the ingredients into a spray bottle. Shake well to mix.

- *To Use*: Spray the oven liberally and let it sit for about 15 minutes.

- Wipe it clean with a cloth or sponge. Rinse and let it air dry.

- *To Store*: Store the leftovers for up to two weeks. Shake to combine before using.

Manual Cleaning Ovens: Not Kid-Friendly: For tougher stains, you can use a commercial oven cleaner. You can also use a ½ cup of household ammonia. Place the ammonia in a shallow pottery/glass container in the cold oven overnight. The burned-on food and grease will become loosened from the ammonia fumes.

Note: Don't turn on the oven while the ammonia is inside of the oven.

Self-Cleaning Ovens: You are fortunate if you have a self-cleaning oven, but it also makes a mess with the ash left behind - similar to cigarette ashes. Clean up is simply wiping the ashes off the surfaces. If you don't want to spend the extra time (anywhere from one to three hours) with an oven pumped up to 880 degrees; there is another way to clean those pesky spills.

Steam Cleaning Method: Choose the steam cleaning cycle which takes about 30 minutes.

- All you need to do is place one cup of water on the bottom of a cool oven.

- Close the door and click the Steam Clean Cycle.

The door won't automatically lock, and it doesn't involve any harsh chemicals. You also clean the racks while still in the oven. Wipe up the moisture and food debris and you are done!

Additional Helpful Usage Oven Tips:

- Never use commercial oven cleaners or liners of any type in or around any part of your self-cleaning oven.

- Don't use aluminum foil to catch any spillage.

- Depending on the model the racks and pans might need to be removed. (Stainless steel must be removed.)

Countertops & The Backsplash

Remove everything from the counters and thoroughly wipe down all of the surfaces using an all-purpose cleaner. Don't forget the backsplash; it needs a good scrubbing also.

Special Countertops

If you have white countertops, a cleaner with bleach included or soft-scrub (see the recipe) can be used for stubborn stains. Be sure to follow the manufacturer's instructions, so you don't damage the surfaces. These are the basics for four common countertops:

Stone Countertops: (Slate, Limestone, & Soapstone):

What You Need:

- Warm, soapy water
- A mild bleach solution
- Or a non-abrasive cleaner

    Note: Be sure to test a spot before you use anything other than warm, soapy water.

    Grease Buildups: Use a mixture of white vinegar and water or an all-purpose cleaner.

You can also use a small brush such as a toothbrush to clean around the edges of

the counters. Never use an abrasive pad because it will scratch the surface.

Butcher-Block Countertops:

What You Need:

- Warm, soapy water
- A mild bleach solution
- A non-abrasive kitchen cleaner

How to Clean:

- Use a toothbrush along the edging to remove any debris.
- If the surface feels tacky, use a baking soda and water paste.
- Then, rinse thoroughly.

Ceramic Tile Countertops:

You can use soap and water to clean ceramic tiles, but you need to be sure to rinse them thoroughly because soap can leave a filmy residue behind. Add some vinegar to the water to alleviate this issue. Never use an abrasive pad or cleaner.

Note: Even though the tile doesn't stain easily—the grout will—with bacterial buildup as a result. Use a mild bleach solution and a toothbrush to clean the grout.

Concrete Countertops:

Clean the surface with warm and soapy water. Rinse it thoroughly. You can use a mild bleach solution, but never use a scouring pad or abrasive cleaner on the surfaces.

For stubborn stains, make a paste of baking soda and water. You may also use talc mixed with a mixture of bleach, ammonia, or hydrogen peroxide. Apply the paste to the stained area, and use a soft brush to scrub the stain gently. Rinse thoroughly.

Marble Countertops:

Cleaning marble countertops is a bit different. It should be cleaned regularly with a soft, damp cloth (microfiber works well) to prevent streaks. Rinse it thoroughly to remove any residue. Wipe it dry because air drying can create water spots.

If acidic foods stain the surface such as wine, orange juice, or tomatoes; you may need to have the professionals clean the spot.

The Cutting Board

You have two choices to remove the leftover stains and smells on your cutting board using natural products. Use a lemon to scrub the board down. You can also sprinkle some baking soda on the surface to remove some of the odors. Just rinse the board later and let it dry. You can also purchase plastic cutting boards that come in several colors for each type of food you would cut.

Cabinets - Drawers & Shelves

Use a damp rag to clean any spills, spots, or splatters with an all-purpose cleaner. If you have wooden cabinets; use some Murphy's Oil Soap, so the wood isn't damaged. However, if the cabinets are new, it is best to ask the manufacturer or builder what works best on your particular cabinet.

Copper Pots

Copper pots hanging in a kitchen makes it have a charming, homey effect. Not only that, but it also saves a lot of space. However, you want to keep the surfaces shiny. Try one of these natural remedies that might surprise you:

- *Catsup:* Give catsup a whirl; it will look really gross, but the acid will help cut through the tarnished surface.

- *Apple Cider Vinegar:* Pour some AC vinegar into a paper plate and let it soak. Rinse the pan and dry it completely.

- *Lemons & Salt:* Cut the lemon into wedges; dip a wedge into the salt, and rub the pan until it's clean. Rinse the pan quickly and thoroughly in cold water, and wipe it dry.

- *Beer:* Put some beer on the pot. Let it sit for a couple of minutes. Rinse and wipe it until dry and shiny.

- *Cottage Cheese:* This is a cure that works without any scrubbing. Leave a layer of cottage cheese on the bottom for approximately five minutes. Rinse it completely and dry.

Stained Coffee Mugs:

If you have stained coffee mugs, try this solution:

- Use sea salt or coarse salt mixed with a little lemon juice and scrub.

- Also, try baking soda and water made into a paste.

- This also works well on stained tea cups or coffee mugs, and even the cutting board.

Chapter 3:
Make the Bathroom Sparkle

Before you begin your deep clean in the bathroom, it's important to clean out the medicine cabinet also. If you have a little toddler who is a lover of climbing, you must take some extra precautions when you stash your medications. Let's think about that for a minute!

Purge the Medicine Cabinet

You already have the medicine cabinet empty from giving it a thorough cleaning; now it's time to do the tedious job of checking the dates of the medicine from the cabinet. Throw away all expired prescriptions or over-the-counter medicines. If you have any ointments, also check them for spoilage.

As crazy as it sounds, your medicine should not be stored in the bathroom because the vitamins and medicines can become damaged from the steam and heat from showers. Place them in the kitchen instead, for safety purposes. It is the safest space, so your toddler doesn't have easy access to drugs.

Store your antiseptics, bandages, gauze, or other first aid items in the medicine cabinet. You can use it to store extra swabs, nail clippers, or any smaller items. Consider placing your toothbrushes in the cabinet to keep them more sanitary.

Place a couple of hangers on the linen closet door for hanging blow dryers, curling irons, or extra towels. It all improves the appearance of the bathroom.

Mirrors

Clean your mirrors and windows using a 50/50 solution of water and vinegar. Many people will use a newspaper or cup up t-shirts. Try not to use paper towels since they will leave behind a residue. The best cleaning product is a microfiber cloth. Use one wet and one dry for polishing.

Drawers

Remove all of the items from the bathroom drawers and place them in containers for sorting. If an item is obviously trash, throw it away immediately. At this point, don't linger on an item. Clean the drawer, so it can thoroughly dry overnight.

Countertops & Sinks

Use the same procedures as used in the kitchen space. It will depend on the material used on the sinks and countertops.

Don't forget to soak the brush holder. Fill the canister with warm—soapy water and let it soak for a few minutes. Dump the dirty water into the toilet and rinse the container with hot water. You can also bleach it if necessary.

The Shower Curtain

It is beneficial to use a shower curtain liner made from cotton, hemp, synthetic, or vinyl. While you are deep cleaning, either replace the liner or machine-wash it in hot water with mild laundry detergent. Washing the liner weekly will help prevent the buildup of mold or mildew. If you prefer to hand-wash the liner, use 1 part bleach to 10 parts of water.

Clean the outer shower curtain by following the manufacturer's instructions or in warm/hot water with a mild detergent.

Note: Leave the shower curtain closed when it is not being used, so water cannot sit in the folds.

Clean the Shower & Tub

Some heavy-duty products may be necessary to remove mildew stains and soap scum build-ups. If you have a shower caddy—it could be time for a replacement—or you can remove it and wash it. You can use a toothbrush for cleaning any small spaces such as the tub jets.

For the shower walls and sides of the tubs, use a mild abrasive and a sponge or cloth. Don't use a brush inside the tub because it can scratch the surface.

Tile Grout: Mix 1 part water and 3 parts baking soda mixed into a paste. Apply to grout and let sit. Spray the area with a vinegar and water solution. Scrub with a toothbrush. After the cleaner finishes foaming; rinse with plain water.

For Deeper Stains: The nasty grout can be tackled with a mixture of 1 part bleach, ten parts water, and a soft bristled brush.

Clean the Shower Head: Use an old toothbrush and bathroom cleaner (such as the new version of Soft-Scrub) to clean the shower head. If you have mineral deposits blocking the holes, you can soak the showerhead using a rubber band, a plastic bag, and white vinegar.

This method works well with heads made from stainless steel, chrome, or other protected metal surfaces.

- Slip the rubber band over the top of the showerhead (loop the band around the arm at least twice so the bag will remain in place).

- Wait for one hour.

- Remove the bag and rinse with water.

- Polish with a soft rag.

If the vinegar solution isn't sufficient, you will need to remove the showerhead for more extensive cleaning. Use the following process to make the job a little simpler:

Disconnect the Showerhead:

- Cushion your tool with a cloth as you work, so the surface finish is protected.

- Use a screwdriver to remove the nut at the shower arm.

- Rinse the showerhead under a faucet (upside down) to remove any loosened debris.

- Dismantle and clean the shower head. If you still see buildups; use a toothbrush, safety pin, or toothpick to poke out any leftover deposits.

- Soak the parts in vinegar overnight.

Thoroughly rinse the showerhead in the morning.

Reassemble and install the showerhead.

- Wrap new plumbing tape around the threads of the shower arm for a good seal.

- Reattach the head to the shower arm with a wrench.

- Use a soft towel or rag to prevent damage.

How to Clean the Faucet & Toilet Handle

Many professionals recommend using disposable disinfecting wipes for the faucet and handle to reduce bacteria buildups greatly. Several studies provided facts indicating that the bacteria found on the toilet set are some of the same germs tested in the kitchen sink.

What a terrible thought, but cross contamination can really happen. If you use a cloth cleaning rag in the bathroom, be sure it doesn't get washed with the same towels used in your kitchen. Think of the vicious circle of bacteria, from the kitchen to the bathroom, before you wash your hands!

Use toothpaste as a scouring agent or multipurpose cleaner. It will shine the faucet, remove crayons from the wall, and serve many other purposes. Think of that when you start getting to the bottom of the tube. Why not try it and be frugal? You might use it from then on!

Super-Scrub for The Toilets:

- Pour ¼ Cup Chlorine Bleach

    OR

- Pour ½ Cup White Vinegar into the bowl.

Don't use either product at the same time. Let the product used sit for about an hour. Brush the entire interior with the brush and flush.

Cleaner for Limescale: Sometimes, Coca-Cola will remedy the issue of limescale buildups. The cola's natural acids will breakdown the lime deposits. Pour the end of a glass of cola into the toilet, swish it around with the toilet brush, and see if it helps. The stains might be too deep, but many have reported the Coca-Cola does work!

However, at any rate, you can begin the cleaning process of the toilet by pouring a cupful of baking soda into the toilet bowl. Let the soda soak for a few minutes. Use a stiff bristle brush and scrub the toilet as needed. Flush. If you still have some difficult spots, you probably need to use a damp pumice stone. It is abrasive but gentle enough not to damage the surface.

The toilet brush should also be thoroughly cleaned after each use to prevent from spreading the bacterial germs. After you have cleaned the bowl, secure the handle of the brush between the bowl and the seat. Pour some bleach over the bristles and let it soak for a few minutes. Rinse it with a bucket of water.

It's essential to keep a clean toilet at all times. Imagine how the bowl releases particles/bacteria into the air each time it is flushed. It is similar to a fireworks display. If the bacteria lingers, you could get sick from salmonella or E. coli as it flies around or lands on the handle and seat.

It is best to close the lid before you flush. It is also best to store contact lenses and toothbrushes in the cabinet. Think about it; it's a risky health practice that has been performed for years. It's about time to change.

Towel Racks & The Hand Towels

Always use the sanitize setting on your washing machine or bleach the towels. Replace them every three or four days. Think of this as you are stripping the bathroom for its deep cleaning. Why not rewash all of the towels for a clean start?

Thoroughly clean the towel bar. If possible, don't install the towel rack near the toilet. Think of the germs, especially with a moist towel. In the future, be sure to use a towel bar so the towel can thoroughly dry. With a crumpled towel, the moisture can create bacteria.

The Ventilation Fan

The bathroom vent fan can sometimes be overlooked, and it's a huge mistake because it could be circulating a lot of dust and possible mold spores from the bathroom.

Step 1: The safest thing to do first is to trip the circuit breaker. Use a tool to remove the protective cover. Prepare a container of hot water with dishwashing soap and let the cover soak.

Step 2: Use the nozzle attachment on the vacuum cleaner to remove the gunk from the fan blades and other nooks and crannies. Use a clean paintbrush to remove the debris from the motor.

Step 3: Wash and rinse the cover.

Step 4: Replace the cover.

Refresh the Space

To finish off the bathroom space, choose a corner of the closet and add a container of baking soda to help absorb any of the musky odors which can collect.

Avoid using products including Lysol or Febreze because they do have a host of chemicals that could be harmful to your toddler. Go natural with one of these choices:

What You Need:

- White vinegar (.5 cup)
- Pure essential oil - ex. lavender, lemon, grapefruit, or orange
- Water (1.5 cups)

How to Clean:

- Combine each of the ingredients into a spray bottle.
- Shake it well and give your bathroom a quick spray before your guests arrive.

Children's Bath Toys

You can use several containers for the children's playtime adventures. You can use a milk crate or plastic laundry basket for the items. It will keep they neatly stored behind the shower curtain. If you want them hidden away in a closet, be sure they are completely dry to prevent mildew.

Generally, the best way to clean the toys is with soap and water. Otherwise, pour about a ½ cup of white vinegar for each gallon of warm water. Soak the toys about ten minutes and rub gently with a sponge.

If you want to clean squeaky toys, just suck up some of the cleaning solutions, shake, and let it air dry.

What about accidental "poop happens" in the water?

You just need to give the item a super clean (unless you cannot relish the thought of keeping the item). Just drain the tub, rinse it well, and clean with your cleaning products of choice. Squeeze the excess water from the toys and put in a solution of 3 parts hot water and 1 part vinegar. Soak for 10-20 minutes. Rinse thoroughly with hot water and dry. Try not to give your toddler a bath right after a meal!

Chapter 4:
General Living Spaces

We dream of having a clean house — but who dreams of actually doing the cleaning? Marcus Buckingham

Most likely, your living room is in desperate need of a 'strip down' to clean all of the hiding places which have harbored peanuts, candy, and popcorn; and this is not the movie theater! It is time to clean the carpets, clear the shelves, and do a super-clean of the space.

Clean the Living Spaces

You are attempting to touch every single spot in your home for a full clean as quickly and efficiently as possible. Some areas contain the same items, such as windows which can always use a bit of touching up. However, while you are in deep clean mode, remember to clean at least the inside and the sills for a tidy home appearance.

- After you have presorted the room, take all of the knick-knacks to another room and wash them. Take down, and clean all of the picture frames, curtains, or any other items such as blankets. If the items don't need washing, you can hang them out for some fresh air.

- Wash down the window frames, baseboards, door frames, all of the woodwork, and use a broom to dust the ceiling.

- Wipe down the ceiling fans using the same method described for your kitchen.

- Cover all of the surfaces that might have a collection of dust or other debris.

- Depending on how much work is involved in this room; you might need to clean the inside of the windows to remove any fingerprints or other collections of grime.

- Thoroughly wipe down the shelves in the room after you have removed the books and knick-knacks.

- Dust all of the furniture and vacuum the couches and chairs, inside and out. Polish all of the furniture in the room, if needed.

- Move the furniture if possible, vacuum, sweep, mop, and polish the wood floors as you normally would on regular cleaning days.

- Replace the clean, fresh rugs and all of the furniture covers.

- Arrange the magazines and papers neatly if you don't have a shelf. You can use a basket or simply stack them in a neat pile.

- Replace the pictures and knick-knacks.

Place a few candles to light later for some relax at the end the day.

Walls, Landings, & Stairs

The walls should be wiped down with warm soapy water. Don't forget to clean the baseboards. Remove all dust bunnies!

If you have any stairs or landings in your home, you will need to thoroughly clean each step with a whisk broom, a hand-held vacuum or a damp rag. If there are carpet sections, be sure to get along the edges thoroughly.

For all handrails and pickets; wipe each individual piece and around the bottom to remove any dirt that might have been captured.

Note: For all spaces, use the crevice tool and brush attachment of your vacuum cleaner to remove the debris from the edges of the wall/baseboards.

Oil Stains on Carpet: If you have carpeted areas that have oil stains; you can use cat litter or baking soda on it to absorb the oil. Even professionals use this process.

Deep Clean the Couch & Chairs

I make no secret of the fact: I would rather lie on a sofa than sweep beneath it. Shirley Conran

Remove all of the cushions from each piece of furniture. Use the long hose attachment on the vacuum cleaner to remove any dust, lint, or crumbs from upholstered furniture. Be sure to go deep into the edges.

Pet Odors in The Carpet or Furniture

If you have a pet, chances are you have a few problems you need to deep clean. You can sprinkle the animal's area with baking soda, as well as the bed. Be sure to vacuum the soda up before it is tracked throughout the house.

The Ceiling Fans

Since you are cleaning the house from top to bottom; it is best to pull out the vacuum cleaner hose and the broom to remove all of the cobwebs from the ceilings. Don't forget to check the fan since it will be circulating clean, fresh air. A dusty fan can ruin all of your hard work. The process only takes about fifteen minutes.

To clean the blades, this is all you need to do:

- *Step 1:* Tape the fan's switch for safety, so it doesn't accidentally get turned on while you clean the blades.

- *Step 2:* Place some old sheets or a drop cloth on the floor and remove any furniture under the fan. The blanket/drop cloth should cover a radius of approximately two that of the blades of the fan.

- *Step 3:* Use a spray bottle filled with water and 2 tablespoons of distilled white vinegar. Spray the inside of an old/damaged pillowcase and place it under each fan blade.

- *Step 4:* Cover your head with a baseball cap or scarf.

- *Step 5:* Stand on a ladder to place your head above the blades.

- *Step 6:* Slip the pillowcase over each blade to remove the bulk of the dust.

- *Step 7:* Use a clean cloth to dust the lingering dust and the light fixture.

Be sure to perform these steps before you vacuum the floors.

The Heating/AC Vents

Check the heating vents, and remove any buildup of dust in each space of the home. Change the filter.

As preventive maintenance, once each month:

- Vacuum the unit with the crevice tool.

- Remove the cover and soak it in soapy water.

- Scrub it with a soft brush.

Remember to have the ductwork cleaned out about every three to five years.

Electronics & The Computer

Your computer keyboard and mouse, as well as your phone, are other excellent spaces that need to be cleaned regularly and thoroughly. Think of all of the spaces where bacteria can grow. Never use abrasive cleaners on any of the products. Always unplug the item before attempting to clean it to prevent electrical damages. Get in the habit of cleaning them weekly as part of your anti-clutter/cleaning adventure.

Chapter 5:
Dining Area

You don't get anything clean without getting something else dirty. Cecil Baxter

Sanitize the Baby Highchairs & Booster Seats

Even though you wipe the baby's high chair every day, it is clean, but it also needs a deep cleaning every once in a while. If you have a dishwasher, you can place the tray directly in the washer but make sure the washing cycle can reach a minimum of 160° Fahrenheit.

You can also use dishwashing liquid and warm water to clean the entire chair. Use a wet wipe, a swab dipped in mouthwash that contains alcohol, and length of dental floss to clean the gunk from all of the nooks and crannies.

Every few days, wipe the chair with hydrogen peroxide which is a natural disinfectant that will kill the germs but won't leave a residue behind. Do a deep cleaning weekly.

Clean the Table & Chairs

If your table is wood, use a wood cleaner (see the recipe). Clean and polish the dining room table, chairs, and other articles of furniture. Be sure to check underneath the seats. You might need to use a whisk brook to remove some spider webs. You can also use dishwashing liquid and warm water to clean the entire chair.

Gently Clean the Chandelier

If you have a simple pattern; just dust the fixture and light bulbs with an inexpensive paintbrush. It will make the room brighter, and you won't see any webs when it isn't Halloween. If you have one of the types with all of the pretty glass bangles, use this method:

It is best to turn the circuit breaker off in the room where the fixture is located. If it is not possible, be sure to cover the switch plate to ensure the light won't be turned on while you're cleaning.

Place a blanket or tarp under the chandelier before you begin to catch the dust and (hopefully) break the fall if you drop a fragile piece of the glass.

Use a solution of 3 parts warm water and 1 part white vinegar, and mix into a spray bottle. Spray a lint-free cloth with the solution and wipe down the spindle and arms of the chandelier. Use a dry lint-free cloth to buff it dry.

Clean the prisms using a vinegar/water solution sprayed on a cloth. Wear a pair of white/cotton gloves, so you don't leave any smudges. You can purchase the gloves at a thrift shop for a minimal fee or online.

Tip: As you are cleaning the chandelier, be sure to lay out the prisms in a pattern, so you understand which way to place them back on the frame.

Remove all items from the cabinet and clean it. Use some of the wood cleaner to refresh the surface, naturally.

Take just five minutes to do a quick run in the china cabinet. You might be surprised what you end up with in your box of questionable items. Quickly, consider items you can easily part with and place them into a keep—toss—donate stack. Don't be tempted to put it in the attic! Save the heirloom pieces and consider consigning, donating, or gifting the items.

It depends on how much silver you have, whether you clean it for now or wait until you have spare time in your schedule.

Clean the Curtains

Vacuum the curtains using the upholstery attachment. A quick once over should do the trick to remove most of the dust. If they look clean after the vacuum, you can use a lint roller later if a touchup is needed.

You have several options for thorough cleaning. You can use the delicate cycle on your washing machine or hand-wash the curtains. It will depend on the sturdiness, quality, as well as the material of the fabric. Check the labels before you proceed.

Chapter 6:
Laundry Area

Have you ever taken anything out of the clothes basket because it had become, relatively, the cleaner thing? Kathrine Whitehorn

Deep-Clean the Laundry Room

Your laundry room might serve as a multi-tasking spot. If you are like many people, the room serves as a storage spot for snacks, gifts, gift wrap, spare batteries, supplies, pet supplies, light bulbs, and so many other items. Are there better spots for any of these items?

Remember; don't hesitate as you begin the purging process. If the item is to be moved, place it in the keep box, and move it to its correct room after the space is cleaned. Thoroughly clean out the cabinets and room of all items except for the washer and dryer. However, that will also be cleaned.

The Washer

Materials Needed:

- White Vinegar (for a natural source) or Bleach
- Baking Soda
- Microfiber Cloth
- Tooth Brush

Step 1: Select the hottest water setting and fill the washer to the highest load size, and the longest wash cycle.

Step 2: As the washer is filling, add one cup of bleach and one quart of white vinegar.

Step 3: Add one cup of baking soda. Close the washer's lid, and agitate for approximately one minute.

Step 4: Let the water, vinegar, and baking soda (or bleach) soak in the tub for about an hour. It is easy just to leave the top open.

Step 5: While the tub is soaking, remove any removable parts for a soak. Don't forget the bleach and fabric softener cups if they are removable. After they are rinsed and dried, you can replace them.

Step 6: Use a small brush such as a toothbrush to clean the topmost part of the agitator and other difficult spaces to reach spots.

Step 7: Clean the sides and top of the machine lid.

Step 8: After one hour of soaking, close the lid, and let the cycle run its course.

Step 9: You can clean around all of the dials with a vinegar solution.

Step 10: Repeat one more hot wash with another quart of vinegar to clear away any loosened residue left from the first wash/rinse cycle.

Step 11: After the washer completes its cycle, wipe the bottom and sides of the washing tub with a vinegar mixture to remove any lingering residue.

Tip: Leave the lid open to allow a thorough drying out to prevent mildew.

Clean the Dryer

The first step is to remove the lint filter and give it a thorough cleaning. Use a duster in the filter well to retrieve the lint out of the trap. You can also use the vacuum cleaner's narrow wand/crevice tool for speedier cleanup time.

Wipe all surfaces with a white vinegar solution.

Check the duct work behind the dryer. Use a vacuum to remove all of the lint and dust. Check the outside of the vent to be sure the flap can move freely. If not, the lint will block the vent and be a possible fire hazard.

Wash the exterior of the dryer with warm, sudsy water. Rinse the soap residue away by using a clean damp rag. Use a dry one to shine the surface.

Chapter 7:
The Children's Corner

"Toddlers are Germ-Warfare Machines in a Cute Package" Debora Geary

The Bedroom Space:

The best plan includes removing all items from under the bed (dust bunnies included). Ideally, under the bed storage is good for those who are limited to space but we tend to forget what is under the lurking space!

Strip and clean the curtains to refresh the room. If you are considering a remodel, have a new pattern ready to hang with your nicely cleaned area. Choose a color scheme and stick with it.

The Bed:

Strip the bed down to the mattress. It is essential to vacuum the mattress and bed springs to remove the dead skin, dust, and dust mites. Be sure to vacuum the perimeter of the bed, which is the haven for mites.

Remove all of the bed linens and wash them. (Pillowcases should be done weekly and the bed protectors should be washed monthly.)

For blankets, decide whether it is a washable, dry clean only, or leave it as it is. If it is clean, it will be okay.

Most pillows are machine washable—and should be washed seasonally to remove any lingering odors, stains, mold, or bacteria.

Designate a spot in the closet or a hidden corner for dirty clothes until laundry day. Be sure all of the items are dry before you stow them away or you could have moldy clothing. Ideally, take them to the laundry room if space permits.

How to Hang Clothes:

Once you have everything in clean order, be sure you hang your items correctly. Try this method:

- Similar colors together
- Hang the sweaters together
- Shirts together
- Pants and skirts together
- Dresses together

Remove the hangers to the laundry room. Don't leave the tangled mess on the floor or occupying precious hanging spaces. Besides, it looks messy.

Clean Up Time at Children's Corner

If you allow a toy box in the living room, you need to provide an attractive container for the items. Sort through the box with the same routine as you do in the bedrooms with the boxes of keep—store—donate—and trash.

Once you have decided which ones to keep; clean them with warm soapy water. You will need to hand-wash the ones that cannot be submerged in water. Use regular dish soap.

Sanitize the Toys:

- Use household liquid chlorine bleach; in one quart of water use 1 tablespoon of bleach or a ¼ cup of bleach in one gallon of water. By diluting the bleach, the chlorine will evaporate within a few minutes. It is considered non-toxic at that point.

- Small plastic toys can be placed in the dishwasher, but be sure there are no batteries in the items. Let them air-dry on a dish rack.

Clean Up with Your Toddler:

- Limit the number of toys. You will take much less time to pick up and keep the spaces clean.

- Contain the clutter wisely in storage bins.

- Schedule clean up with your toddler (Good luck!)

- Start your toddler young of how to pick up his/her toys. However, don't set unrealistic goals. Maybe start with pulling the blanket over the bed or putting shoes in the proper spaces. Start small.

- Your youngster is learning, so give specific instructions. You must capture attention because of short attention spans. Begin using a color code game. Indicate you are picking up everything yellow for example. Continue as long as the strategy works.

- Plan a special activity after cleaning up the chosen toddler space.

Ways to Keep Your House Clean With A Toddler

Establish Rules for Playtime: It's important to teach your kid they should put toys away before moving onto the next event. Depending on the ages and temperament of your baby will be the judge of this step as a success.

All toys have a proper space. It is a good practice to teach your baby where the toys belong. For the den area, try designating a toy box of favorites so you can enjoy a bit of TV while your youngster explores the goodies.

Prompt bad behavior with the removal of toys. If your child absolutely refuses to help clean his/her play corner, say it is sad, but a particular item will be stashed until it is clean. Teach logic of good behavior equals great rewards (return of the toy).

Create a put-away basket. This can be useful for your toddler as well as other family members. Make it a fun game. That usually works, especially if a treat is at the end of chore time.

Conclusion:
A Final Word

Thank you for making it through to the end of *Home Cleaning Tips*. Let's hope it was informative and provided you with all of the tools you need to achieve your goals whatever they may be.

Lastly - Get Organized

Store your supplies in easily accessible areas such as on the laundry room top shelf away from your toddler. You will want to include items including baking soda in a shaker container, a multipurpose cleaner, vinegar and water, and hydrogen peroxide. Place a window cleaner somewhere in your den for quick cleanups. Store cleaning rags in the same space.

Create A Cleaning Routine

Daily Schedule:

Sweep the Floors: Take a few extra minutes out of your day to do a dry sweep of the most used rooms including the kitchen or mudroom. A dustpan and broom take up very little room in the pantry. You are there in a flash when the crumbs from the table or pet hair collect under the table.

Declutter by The Day: It is simpler to do a quick declutter of items such as sales papers, clothes, toys, and other less used items taking up space. Involve everyone in the process from Legos to you file cabinets (if you have one). Give your toddler a chore of five minutes to embrace the game of 'put away.'

Wipe All Countertops: Even though you wash out the sink after doing dishes, it's also important to use dish soap to deep-clean the surfaces. Do the same over each of the bathroom spaces to make your weekly cleanup much quicker.

Do Laundry: Do at least one load of laundry daily, especially with a toddler. You should do the entire process from washing, drying, folding, and putting away. Not only are you removing bacteria ridden clothing, but you are also eliminating the cluttered items throughout the house.

Weekly Chores

Monday: Clean the Bathrooms: It is a great idea to choose Monday for deep cleaning the bath area, especially if you have a busy lifestyle. Clean all surfaces except for the floors; including the mirrors, toilet, shower/tub, and countertops.

Tuesday: Dusting Day: Take about 15 to 20 minutes to dust. Be sure to use a long-handled want to reach all of the high corners and spaces. Try not to leave any spider webs. If you have toddlers, they can join in with a dusting mitt. Children are never too young to learn unless they still put everything in his/her mouth!

Wednesday: Vacuum Day: Deodorize the room while you vacuum. Add a drop or two of your favorite essential oil on a cotton ball to the bag or canister to add a delicate aromatherapy to your vacuuming routine.

Thoroughly vacuum all of the floor surfaces. Move furniture that isn't too heavy. Use the crevice attachment and do the edges of the room. You can also hit the corners for any lurking webs which might have been missed on dusting day.

Start in the center of the room. Vacuum vertically and horizontally. Yes, you are vacuuming twice, but you are ensuring you have covered all of the flooring - especially the carpet where bits of food and debris can hide. If you have a pet, the double vacuum will also remove any pet dander and hair. You will love the lines left by the vacuum, letting you know it's done right.

Thursday: Wash the Floor Surfaces: Clean all of the tile and vinyl floors using a steam mop. Use warm water and vinegar along with a couple of drops of clove and lemon essential oils on the hardwood floors.

Friday: Variety Day: Get the rest of the spaces you missed. Go do your grocery shopping or complete another task in your home. This is considered your 'optional' work day. You could clean the silver.

Saturday: Wash All Sheets & Towels: Concentrate on these items instead of 'regular' laundry. Use the special powdered laundry detergent to make them fresh and soft.

Sunday: Basic Day: Sunday is a time of relaxation and rest for most. Do your four daily tasks (declutter, wipe the counters, do a load of laundry, and sweep the floors).

Staying on-task takes a routine such as this one. Once you have a set pattern, it will become normal and not seem so daunting. Eventually, you will be comfortable doing the manageable tasks to give yourself a sense of accomplishment and make the home run smoothly.

How to Do A Quick Touch-Up

Start your touch-up plan early in the day before you have a chance to be 'too tired' or decide to do it tomorrow. Start while you are waiting for the coffee/tea and move the items around and spray a bit of all-purpose cleaner for a clean aroma.

Begin in one part of the house just as you did with day one. This is a brief list of what you will need to do to condition and group all of your hard work into one beautiful setting.

Pick up all of the items that don't belong in the rooms and place them in a basket. Call your family members attention to the container, and instruct them to put the items in their correct places.

Change all of the sheets and rotate the blankets: It has been a week, and it is a perfect time to start your latest habit as you keep a tidy home. Bed sheets should be washed in warm/not hot water (unless specified otherwise on the label). Keep the bed made daily for an organized, relaxing area.

Windex the glasses/windows using the plan of one room/space at a time. Finish one space and move onto the next.

Sanitize the remotes and telephones with a disinfecting wipe.

Vacuum or damp mop the floors. Place all of the clean runners, mats, and throw rugs into the cleaned designated areas.

Quick dust over of each space since dust quickly gathers. Start with the furniture (tables, bookshelves, and dressers). Use a microfiber cloth to wipe down the electronics (cable box, television, stereo, and the computer).

Check the ceiling fans or chandeliers for any clusters of dust. Use an extension duster for the recessed lighting or any other high areas. Check the pictures at the same time because a quick sweep with the duster should be all that is necessary.

Now you have it, and it wasn't that hard. You will have a routine soon, so cheer; up and get cleaning. I hope you enjoy all of the great products and a clean house for a bonus! Lastly, if you found this book useful in any way, a review on Amazon is always appreciated!

Index

Chapter 1: Go with Natural Cleaning Products

Essential Homemade Cleaning Containers

Natural Cleaning Products

- Baking Soda
- White Vinegar
- Hydrogen Peroxide
- Liquid Castile Soap
- Natural Dish Soap
- Borax
- Microfiber Cloths
- Microfiber Cloth Mops
- Sponges
- Scrub Brushes
- Squeegee
- Broom & Mop
- Dusting Wands
- Vacuum Cleaner with Attachments
- Essential Oils
- Caddies or Tool Containers

Clean the Couches & Chairs

- Cleaner for Fabric Furniture

Other Natural Cleaners for The House

Lemon & Clove Liquid Dish Soap

Lemon Dishwasher Powder - Detergent

Disinfectant Wipes

All-Purpose Cleaner

Glass Cleaner

Vinegar Clean Up in A Bottle

Lemon Household Cleaner

Lemon Juice for Stubborn Stains

Soft Abrasive Cleaners

Vinegar for Limescale

Natural Toilet Bowl Scrubber

Homemade Drain Cleaner

- Product 1: Clear the Drain
- Product 2: Drain Freshener

Clear Away Rust Spots

Natural Wood Cleaner

Dusting Spray for Cleaning Furniture

Carpet Cleaning

- Nontoxic Alternatives
- Carpet Freshener

Chapter 2: Cleaning Kitchen Spaces

The Kitchen Sink

- Porcelain Sinks
- The Garbage Disposal

Sanitizing the Sponges

Clean Small Appliances

- Toasters
- Can Opener
- The Blender

Clean the Microwave

Clean the Refrigerator

Super-Clean the Oven

Natural Oven Cleaner: Option 1-3

Manual Cleaning Ovens: Not Kid-Friendly

Self-Cleaning Ovens

Steam Cleaning Method

Additional Helpful Usage Oven Tips

Countertops & The Backsplash

Special Countertops

- Stone Countertops (Slate, Limestone, & Soapstone)
- Butcher-Block Countertops
- Ceramic Tile Countertops
- Concrete Countertops
- Marble Countertops

The Cutting Board

Cabinets, Drawers & Shelves

Copper Pots

    Stained Coffee Mugs

Chapter 3: Make the Bathroom Sparkle

Purge the Medicine Cabinet

Mirrors

Drawers

Countertops & Sinks

The Shower Curtain

The Shower & Tub

- Tile Grout
- Clean the Shower Head

How to Clean the Faucet & Toilet Handle?

- Super-Scrub for The Toilets
- Cleaner for Limescale

Towel Racks & The Hand Towels

The Ventilation Fan

Refresh the Space

Children's Bath Toys

Chapter 4: General Living Spaces

Clean the Living Spaces

Walls, Landings, & Stairs

- Oil Stains on Carpet

Deep Clean the Couch & Chairs

Pet Odors in The Carpet or Furniture

The Ceiling Fans

The Heating/AC Vents

Electronics & The Computer

Chapter 5: Dining Area

Sanitize the Baby Highchairs & Booster Seats

Clean the Table & Chairs

Gently Clean the Chandelier

Spruce the China Cabinet - Hutch & Buffet

Clean the Curtains

Chapter 6: Laundry Area

Deep-Clean the Laundry Room

- The Washer
- Clean the Dryer

Chapter 7: The Children's Corner

The Bedroom Space

Clean Up Time at Children's Corner

- Sanitize the Toys
- Clean Up with Your Toddler

Ways to Keep Your House Clean With A Toddler

Conclusion: A Final Word

- Lastly - Get Organized
- Create A Cleaning Routine
- Daily Schedule
- Weekly Chores
- How to Do A Quick Touch-Up

Description

Do you have little people under your feet every day? Are you unsure of what cleaning products to use for safety?

Home Cleaning Tips will help you eliminate much of the stress involved with cleaning with your precious children in mind.

These are just a few of the topics discussed:

- Essential Homemade Cleaning Containers
- Natural Cleaning Products
- How to Clean Kitchen Spaces?
- How to Make the Bathroom Sparkle?
- How to Clean Your Living Spaces?
- How to Super-Clean the Dining Area
- Cleaning the Laundry Space
- The Children's Corner Specialty
- This is just the beginning!

These are several cleaners you can make at home:

- Dusting Spray for Cleaning Furniture

- Lemon & Clove Liquid Dish Soap

- Lemon Household Cleaner

- Natural Toilet Bowl Scrubber

- Disinfectant Wipes

- So Much More!

There is no need to purchase all of those high-priced cleaning products when you can prepare your own in the convenience of your home any time you need them. All you need is a few essential items which are fully explained.

Don't live in a dirty house for another day. Why not add this to your personal cleaning library now?

CPSIA information can be obtained
at www.ICGtesting.com
Printed in the USA
LVHW021757050520
655000LV00014B/4203